URBAN MYTHS

ANTON & NO CYCLE

Photograph from *Anton* by Molly Shinhat.
Photograph from *No Cycle* by Ken Gregg.

Cover artwork by Mary Standjofski.
Book design & typesetting by Karen Haughian.

Printed and bound in Canada by Hignell Printing Ltd.
Published with the assistance of The Canada Council.
Dépôt légal, Bibliothèque nationale du Québec and the National Library of Canada.

Canadian Cataloguing In Publication Data
Main entry under title:
Urban myths : Anton & No cycle

(Performance series)
ISBN 0-921833-15-6

I. Title   II. Title: Anton   III. Title: No cycle.   IV. Series.

PS8587 . T297U73 1992   C812' . 54   C92-090708-3
PR9199 . 7 . S83U73 1992

NuAge Editions, P.O. Box 8, Station E, Montreal, Quebec, H2T 3A5

URBAN MYTHS

ANTON & NO CYCLE

HARRY
STANDJOFSKI

NUAGE
EDITIONS

Introduction

Harry Standjofski is not only a fine writer; he is equally well known as an actor and director. The quality he brings to his writing obtains, to a degree, from his ability to see theatre in all of its aspects. How will this piece of writing work for an actor? How will a director be able to deal with the subplot? How will it all work together?

Theatre imbues Standjofski's life. He watches life to see how it will play on stage. He writes constantly, so that his plays never contradict real life, though they do look at it from a unique viewpoint. For example, it really did snow on October 18, 1989, as his characters tell us in *Anton*. It's not even an important factor in the story—it's just that Standjofski likes to be precise in creating his urban mythology.

Standjofski has some strong opinions about theatre. One is that theatre should be theatre, and not a possible movie or television program. It should work on stage, and not anywhere else. These two plays, both built on older traditions of theatre, exemplify that belief.

Standjofski for years has described *No Cycle* as a work in progress. It has received stage productions and critical acclaim; it's a well-crafted and hilarious piece. It got that way through the long process of working on it with actors. Standjofski is thankful that a core group works with him while he is developing a play. *No Cycle* was worked over a long period and *Anton* was developed over several months with the actors before the official rehearsal period started.

All of Standjofski's writing works on a number of levels, and one that cannot be discounted is the personal. While his writing is universal, there are resonances from his own life that continue to sound in other people's lives as well.

Traditional Noh plays are performed on a bare stage, and production is simple. As they are part of Zen Buddhism, they are austere. Movement is often symbolic of something else—rain, wind, drinking, or weeping. This may be too difficult for Western audiences—Standjofski's characters actually weep.

Traditional Noh theatre does not demand that the five plays have a common topic, but they must provide a progression of mood and tempo.

The God play, for example, is celebratory; the warrior play, stirring; the woman play is softly melancholy, the madwoman play is dramatic and the auspices play is energetic.

There are those who believe that it is blessed to tell religious stories and at the same time make the listeners laugh. While Standjofski is probably not trying to give us Christian teachings in *No Cycle*, he is making profound observations about life, about how there are ways of avoiding the traps of our own making. And he certainly makes us laugh while he goes through the stations of the cross in the *Rabbit* play; and he ends with the second most important date of the Christian calendar—the birth of Christ.

A play that begins with Easter and ends with Christmas; a play that deals with death and love and Chekhov. It makes us laugh, and there is lots to think about. It couldn't exist anywhere but in the theatre. What more could we ask?

Nothing more than another play about Chekhov, sort of. *Anton* is a play about wealth. Money can't buy happiness. Social position is no guarantee of security. And again we have religious comment—this time around the harvest festival of Thanksgiving.

You can enjoy Standjofski's plays simply for what is said in the script. You can have a wonderful time with the little background jokes—in *Anton*, the salutes to Chekhov. The Three Sisters are there, the cherry orchard is compressed into one invisible tree, and nobody goes to Moscow. But it matters not if the reader has never read a play by Chekhov: the play is what it says it is—a look at a bourgeois family. In North America, we often forget that Chekhov's plays are as full of comedy as pathos; Standjofski never forgets the human comedy.

By laughing at a madwoman, a man who cannot love and the other characters in this play, do we learn compassion? Maybe not, but we learn of Standjofski's compassion for humankind. His is not mocking laughter, but the laughter of the Zen monk who awakens us, who tries to awaken us, with a koan—a puzzle with no answer.

Janet Coutts
Montreal
October 1992

ANTON

Anton was first presented in Montreal by Point of View Productions at the Strathearn Theatre in October 1991 with the following cast:

Robert	Robert Higden
Nikolai & Robert's friend	Roch Lafortune
Maria	Maria Bircher
Suzanna & Irina	Susan Glover
Paulina	Pauline Little
Director	Harry Standjofski
Set design	Allison Moore
Lighting	David d'Anjou
Stage managers	Teresa Kaeser & Johanne Pomrenski

Anton was workshopped by Theatre YMX in November 1990. Special thanks to Robert Parson for his work in the creation of the role of Nikolai.

THE CHARACTERS
Seen:

Robert	Mid-thirties
Maria	Early thirties
Nikolai	Mid- to late thirties
Suzanna	Late twenties
Paulina	Mid-thirties

Unseen:

Robert's friend	Mid-thirties
Irina	Mid-thirties

THE PLACE
Montreal

THE TIME
October 1989

An intermission is suggested after Scene 8.

SCENE 1

> *Sunday, October 1, 1989, 6:00 p.m. The phone room. Robert on the phone by a window, shadow of his friend on the other end.*

Robert: Listen, have I changed much?

Friend: How do you mean?

Robert: How long have we known each other?

Friend: Have you changed since...

Robert: Yeah, since you've known me.

Friend: ...oh, yes...

Robert: Well, how?

Friend: What is that sound?

Robert: Eh? Oh, that. Sirens. There's a fire across the street.

Friend: A what?

Robert: You remember the old folks' home? It's burning.

Friend: Big fire?

Robert: Lots to burn there—lots of rich old folks' money, ha. Actually, the money hasn't even started to burn, just the interest, ha, ha.

Friend: You guys safe?

Robert: Oh, yeah. The hydro's out, but—

Friend: No, I mean the fire—

Robert: No, no, I was worried about the big tree catching, but they seem to have it under control—get back to my question.

Friend: Have you changed?

Robert: Mm-hm...

Friend: I don't know...you're older.

Robert: And you're a genius.

Friend: What do you want me to say? Is this why you called?

Robert: I guess.

Friend: Out of the blue: "Have I changed?"

Robert: We're both successful...you know what I mean?

Friend: How have you changed?... You've sagged.

Robert: Sagged.

Friend: Yeah...

Robert: I'm in better shape than you are, buddy.

Friend: That's not what I—I mean sagged...deflated. Your eyes, they're like...weighted down. I don't mean tired...more like you're bored or...like you can't see very far.

Robert: Don't be shy. Say what's on your mind.

Friend: There's a hole, there's a great gash opened up in front of you...so nobody can get too near you anymore—and everything you say or anything anyone says to you just falls into this bottomless gash, gets sucked into it...you still there?

Robert: Yeah...

Friend: I don't know...maybe I'm just talking about myself.

SCENE 2

> *Tuesday, October 3, 1989. 21h30. Art gallery vernissage. Maria and Nikolai in front of a huge painting.*

Nikolai: *(With slight accent.)* Whereas her earlier works were possessed with a rage against the political system under which she strove to create, it is as if since she has been here she...her rage has slowly vanished, replaced with...a complacency... life is so much easier here, and this is the paradox—under oppressive conditions her work was positive—the rage was expressed in a positive manner: "Come, let us fight," that sort of thing...whereas now, now that she is successful—she is in love, her work is being accepted—it is as if this comfort has brought out all that is pessimistic in her. Her work is bleak, imbued with nostalgia—a word that in our language has more melancholic connotations. Here, with nothing to rebel against, this has left her...sad.

Maria: Does she want to go back?

Nikolai: Back?

Maria: To the Soviet Union.

Nikolai: Why should she want to do that?

Maria: She is sadder here.

Nikolai: No, she—

Maria: OK, not sadder, but "nostalgic."

Nikolai: Nostalgic, yes, but happier.

Maria: How can she be happier if her work is bleaker?

Nikolai: Her personal life is happier. The happier she is, the bleaker her artistic vision.

Maria: But maybe at home she'd be happier and—

Nikolai: This is the paradox—

Maria: Wait a minute...

Maria: So is she— *(together)*
Nikolai: You see—

Maria: Pardon me.

Nikolai: Sorry, you were—

Maria: No, please, go ahead. I wasn't going to say anything.

Nikolai: Please.

Maria: Is she in love with you?

Nikolai: I beg your pardon?

Maria: You said she is in love. Is it with you?

Nikolai: What a strange question.

Maria: I mean, you seem to know her, so...

Nikolai: No. It is not I.

Maria: I'm sorry—

Nikolai: No, it's—

Maria: Please, you were going to say—

Nikolai: It is as if—

>   *Enter Robert.*

Robert: All they had left was white.

Maria: Where were you?

Robert: I had to re-park the car—it had been driving me crazy since we got here—I was too close to a hydrant. I knew we should have cabbed it. Parking on Sherbrooke, eh? Here.

Maria: What's this?

Robert: I told you, all they have left is white.

Maria: I hate white wine—you know that.

Robert: It's all they had.

Maria: White wine gives me a headache.

Robert: Well, here.

Maria: I don't want it.

Robert: So what am I going to do with it?

Maria: Drink it.

Robert: It's a Bordeaux.

Nikolai: Would you like my red?

Maria: Oh, no—

Nikolai: Please. I have not touched it. We make a cultural exchange.

Maria: Are you sure? Thank you. Oh, Robert, this is...I have absolutely no idea, ha.

Nikolai: Nikolai.

Robert: Robert Martin.

Maria: I'm Maria Dalton.

            Hellos.

Maria: He's from the Soviet Union.

Robert: You a friend of the artist's?

Nikolai: Yes.

Robert: *(To Maria.)* Listen, I'm sorry.

Maria: What?

Robert: About the wine. I should have remembered.

Maria: It's nothing.

Robert: No, no. I'm sorry. I want you to know that.

Maria: It's all right.

Nikolai: So you are—

Maria: The painter, yes.

Nikolai: No, I was going to ask if you were collectors—if you might purchase one of Ludmilla's paintings.

Maria: Oh...well...it's possible...

Robert: A vague possibility...

SCENE 3

> *Saturday, October 7, 22h30. The kitchen. Suzanna on the phone. Alcohol and cigarettes.*

Suzanna: Well, what time?...well, when will you know?...when do you think you'll know?...so what the fuck am I supposed to do in the meanwhile, masturbate?...ha-ha, you're a laugh riot—why don't you just give me the address? Well, what do you know about this evening? Nothing, right? You're guessing, right? You're stringing me on while I slowly go out of my skull...relax? Relax? What the fuck, what are you, my guru? You piece of shit, you sit there, "relax," what do you know about me? What do you know about me at this moment, Paul? Fuck all. You sit there and I go mad. This is getting serious. I need—wait, no, wait a minute...no...

> *Enter Paulina, in a bathrobe. She sits slowly.*

Suzanna: No, it's nothing, it's...no...no...look, who else is going to be there?...mm-hm...mm-hm...why her? No, I don't mind—no, forget I said anything. It's me, I'm a bitch, remember? I just want to get out of this house...no, Paul, I...yes...

> *Paulina gets up slowly and exits.*

Suzanna: Yes...well, WHEN?...all right...all right...yes...well, make it quick.

> *Hangs up. Re-enter Paulina wearing rubber gloves and carrying a raw turkey on a plate and a knife. Sits and begins to clean out the insides.*

Suzanna: I don't think I'm going to be here tomorrow...who's coming?

Paulina: Robert's side.

Suzanna: What time did you...'cause I'm really not sure if—

Paulina: Around seven.

Suzanna: Yeah, I don't know if I'll be here...anyway, I'll tell you tomorrow... *(To phone.)* Come on, come on. Fuck, I hate waiting around. Are you keeping that? The guts.

Paulina: Yes.

Suzanna: What are you going to do with it?

Paulina: Boil it.

Suzanna: For what?

Paulina: For broth.

Suzanna: Broth for what?

Paulina: Soup.

Suzanna: That's guts. Guts broth. Lovely.

Exit Suzanna with empty glass. Music.

Paulina: Change stations.

Suzanna: *(Off.)* What?

Paulina: I don't want to hear that music. Put on something with no words.

Suzanna: *(Off.)* Look—

Paulina: I don't want to hear any words.

Music changes. Re-enter Suzanna with a glass of alcohol.

Suzanna: Better?... It's cold in here. *(Phone rings.)* Yes, Paul?... Oh, no—no, she's not...no, I don't. Is there a message? I don't know... I have no idea—look, do you want to leave a message?... I assume so—so, do you— What?...I don't know...I just said I don't know—Look, I'm expecting— What! I— Look, just a minute— No, just— *(To Paulina.)* Where's Maria?

Paulina: Opera.

Suzanna: *(To phone.)* She's at the opera... I don't know—late, operas are very long...ok? Goodbye— What?...I don't know, all right? Goodbye...yes— Goodb— *(Hangs up.)* Fucking idiot. I need my own line. This is ridiculous. Next week I'm having one installed. Doesn't it drive you nuts?... My own line...ha, I need my own line...yes, yes, yes...Maria went to the opera with Robert?

Paulina: With the Russian.

Suzanna: Yeah, I was going to say... So who is this Russian guy?

Paulina: I haven't met him.

Suzanna: Is he another in a series of painters?

Paulina: I haven't met him.

Suzanna: What are you doing tonight?

Paulina: Cleaning the turkey.

Suzanna: Pretty scrawny turkey... You should go out. It'd do you some good...get out of this fucking house—this tomb, where we will all die unless we sell it. Which we won't...anyway...can you see this pimple?

Paulina: What pimple?

Suzanna: Good... The days are getting so short. When do we change the clocks, do you know? It's this month, though, isn't it? I love that when the—when it's, you know, pitch dark at 5:30, the night starts. I think sunlight is highly over-rated. I think the outdoors is over-rated. Tans are over-rated, fresh air is over-rated, all health is over-rated.

Paulina starts to cry. Suzanna doesn't notice.

Suzanna: As a matter of fact, I think that, generally speaking, everything, the whole world, is over-rated.

Exit Suzanna with empty glass. Paulina cries. Phone rings.

Suzanna: (*Off.*) You going to get that? Paulina...Paulina, answer it! (*Rushes in.*) What's the matter with you? Hello?

SCENE 4

Tuesday, October 10th, 14h30. Salon. Maria and Nikolai.

Maria: Are you sure you want to leave her?... How long have you and...and...

Nikolai: Irina.

Maria: How long have you been together?

Nikolai: Ten years...

Maria: Ten years... Are you sure you want to leave her? But a relationship does involve work.

Nikolai: Shouldn't love be effortless? Don't you fall in love? It's accidental. It lands on you unexpectedly, like birdshit.

Maria: Oh, Nikolai.

Nikolai: We should not be afraid of these accidents, of change.

Maria: Why did you marry her? If all you want is "change."

Nikolai: I loved her. Then. But I am not afraid of change. I cannot tell who I will love, how or when I will fall.

Maria: Of course it's more fun to "fall"—a ten-year-old relationship can't possibly...compete with the rush of something new.

Nikolai: Marriage is not the end: we pledge eternal love and die.

Maria: Of course not. You have to work at it.

Nikolai: No, I feel it should be effortless. Like breathing.

Maria: Breeding?

Nikolai: Yes, breathing.

Maria: Oh, breathing...

Nikolai: Do you know why they say love is eternal? Because when you love someone, it is forever. That even dead love stays with you, hangs on like a dull pain—like shit to a goldfish.

Maria: You have a peculiar habit of mixing love and excrement.

Nikolai: Eternal love—who believes in those old words anymore?

Maria: I like those old words, simple words. Fidelity. Work. Respect. They're easy to understand.

Nikolai: And passion?

Maria: Oh, I'm so sick of passion—I mean, everything, all the art, the movies, the...I don't know—it's always "passion, passion"—like people are only really in love if they're trying to kill each other at the same time. What about those couples that have gone quietly along for years?

Nikolai: Those couples have their passion.

Maria: I know. I don't mean...passion's important...I don't really know how to phrase it... Passion can be quiet, can't it?

Nikolai: Sometimes it's difficult to distinguish between quiet and dead.

Maria: Like when you see old couples holding hands...that's what I mean...I hate talking about this, I think... Is it really that bad with you and...oh, god—

Nikolai: Irina.

Maria: I'm sorry, I don't know why I have such a hard time remembering her name.

Nikolai: It is dead. There is nothing worse. One should not live with the dead. Maria, how do you reconcile the lack of passion in your life?

Maria: I have my work.

Nikolai: Irina is a writer, a brilliant woman. I do not know why she insists on needing me.

Maria: Anyway, though, I can't say my relationship is totally without passion.

Nikolai: Yes, and how is it with you? Enough talk of me—

Maria: No, really, it's fine... It's been, you know, hotter...he's busy...I'm busy...all relationships have their hills and valleys.

Nikolai: Irina and I are in the desert. No water, no camel. We lie in the heat waiting to die, screaming in each other's ears.

Maria: Oh, Nikolai, ha.

Nikolai: Maria...

Maria: Yes?

Nikolai: You have no children?

Maria: No. Robert has a son from his first marriage, but we hardly see him. He lives in Toronto with his mother.

Enter Paulina, eating a sandwich and holding garden shears.

Maria: Oh, Paulina, this is Nikolai. This is my sister Paulina.

Hellos. Pause.

Maria: What's that you're eating?

Paulina: Turkey sandwich.

Maria: Oh yes, Paulina made us a beautiful Thanksgiving dinner... You once had a job as a cook, didn't you?

Paulina: A summer job. On a cruise ship. It was full of old people. Two of them died. Apparently that's normal. I don't know why old people take tropical cruises. They can't stay in the sun very long. They bitched about everything the whole trip. Of course, they told everybody what a lovely time they had when they got home. But I got to see the Caribbean and that was nice. All that poverty. You must be very happy with what's going on in Hungary.

Nikolai: Oh...yes...it's remarkable.

Paulina: I'm going to cut the dahlias. October's been too cold.

Exit Paulina.

Maria: Isn't she beautiful? I'm sorry, she's been depressed lately. Well, not just lately. Since she moved here. She and her husband separated. But isn't her face beautiful? The sadness.

Nikolai: She lives here with you?

Maria: Yes. I have another sister that lives here as well. Oh, and I have a brother, André. He's in Singapore.

Nikolai: This is such a beautiful room. What kind of tree is that?

Maria: The tree? I'm not sure. It's very old, though.

Nik   A beautiful room. The light. It must be a wonderful place to work. What happened across the street there?

Maria: A fire a couple of days ago. Of course I don't really work in here. I work in my studio.

Nikolai: Oh, but the light is much more beautiful in here.

Maria: You think?

Nikolai: Oh yes. Maria...it is wonderful how I can sit here with you in silence... Do you always wear black?

Maria: What? I guess I do.

Nikolai: I have only ever seen you in black. Has someone died?

Maria: No.

Nikolai: It is becoming to you, but you should try some colour.

Maria: I'll think about it.

Nikolai: She is pregnant.

Maria: Who? Oh. Irina? Do you really think it's impossible to work it out?

Nikolai: Work. Again work. The world is work—I think love is the other thing: effortless, incomprehensible, frightening. What is beautiful is beautiful because it frightens me. I do not understand it. Once I understand it, it is no longer beautiful, it is just...work. Why is this room beautiful, Maria? The light. What is light? We don't know. Oh, of course we can define it scientifically, but...why am I so moved seeing it come through the window? That is what I need: to be moved, to be frightened. Having a child does not frighten me. It bores me, it makes me sick with work. Her child. Her. She who I understand...I am sorry. I burden you with this.

Maria: No, not at all.

Nikolai: I talk...why do I complain? It sounds so lovely: I am going to be a father.

> *Nikolai cries. Maria approaches him slowly, holds him.*

Nikolai: I'm sorry...I hardly know you...this liberty...

Maria: Shh...it's all right...

Nikolai: I feel so comfortable here...to talk with...

Maria: Talk...talk...

> *Enter Paulina, with dahlias, unnoticed.*

Paulina: I see...I see... (Exits.)

Nikolai: How did my life become such a joke?

SCENE 5

> *Friday, October 13, 15h00. Salon. Suzanna on the couch, smoking in the dark. Enter Robert. He opens the curtains.*

Suzanna: Thanks.

Robert: Oh...you're here...I thought I smelled smoke.

Suzanna: (*Blowing her nose—there is blood on her handkerchief.*) You want me to leave?

Robert: No, it's just...we're moving the room.

Suzanna: What?

Robert: Maria's moving her studio in here and the salon will be where her studio is. Do you mind?

Suzanna: I don't give a fuck.

Robert: It'll be great. We'll have a fireplace in the salon now.

> *Suzanna blows her nose.*

Robert: Do you have a cold?

Suzanna: Why are you here?

Robert: I live here.

Suzanna: I mean home. Today.

Robert: I landed a big fish yesterday, Suzanna. I made a lot of money. It was a long haul, but worth it. Over two hundred thousand dollars. So I said to myself: take the day off.

Suzanna: Oh, Robert, you're so impulsive.

Robert: Besides, it's Friday the thirteenth, ha. You want to give us a hand?

Suzanna: Bravo.

Robert: With the move.

Suzanna: You want me to move things. Like, carry things from one room to another.

Robert: Come on now, a little effort.

Suzanna: I made my efforts last night, thank-you-very-much. Where's Maria, anyway?

Robert: Well, obviously she's packing up her studio.

Suzanna: Obviously...oh fuck, you know. I just got up.

Robert: It's three o'clock.

Suzanna: You couldn't hire someone to do this?

Robert: It's a room, Suzanna.

Suzanna: How come I had no say in this?

Robert: "I don't give a fuck."

Suzanna: Any other decisions you've made in my absence?

Robert: I'm sorry, Suzanna.

Suzanna: What?

Robert: No, you're right. We should have consulted you.

Suzanna: Fuck off.

Robert: I mean it. I'm sorry. You live here too.

Suzanna: Am I awake? What the fuck is happening? What?

Robert: It's Friday the thirteenth, ha... Whatever became of the chairs in here?

Suzanna: Chairs.

Robert: Big old leather chairs. They were here when we moved in. In this room. Do you ever think about how maybe inanimate objects have personalities? This room...the chair...doors. We never ask the objects if they want to be moved. Like, I have the hardest time throwing away pens; I use a pen, I write all sorts of things with it—it seems to me that the pen had something to do with the writing of my memos or my cheques or what have you...and when it runs dry then I throw it away—it feels like I'm chucking away a friend.

Suzanna: Am I supposed to respond to this?

Robert: Or—do you ever think this?—I'm raking leaves and one leaf gets left behind and I swear I hear it calling to its friends—I have to go and rake it in with the rest of them...like when I went to a different high school than my friends from elementary school...I hated that. That's how I figure the leaf feels.

Suzanna: Robert, when was the last time you raked leaves?

Robert: We live in the same house, Suzanna, and we hardly know each other. I just thought I'd let you in on what I think about. We're so busy making money and working, I feel sometimes that I've lost the ability to talk...just talk—to just live—you know what I mean? Not work—not have to feel that my life is only justified by my work...but that my life has a value all by itself—just by its existence.

Suzanna: Maybe you should start thinking about your wife. By all accounts, there's a decided lack of sexual activity in her life right now.

Robert: Well...it's true that I have been...busy recently with things outside my control...but I'm sure that now...things will pick up.

Doorbell rings.

Suzanna: You a tiger, Bob. I only regret Maria found you first.

Robert: I'll take this chair. You want to maybe roll up the carpet? I'll see how Maria's doing. *(Exits.)*

Suzanna: *(Beginning to roll the carpet.)* What am I doing here? I can't believe I'm here. Fuck.

    Enter Nikolai with a wrapped painting. Watches Suzanna's butt.

Suzanna: *(Seeing him.)* Oh, hello...the Russian.

Nikolai: I'm sorry? Yes.

Suzanna: I'm Suzanna.

Nikolai: Have we...?

Suzanna: I'm very intuitive.

Nikolai: Ah.

Suzanna: So, what's your name?

Nikolai: I'm sorry, ha...Nikolai.

Suzanna: Nikolai. I didn't think they called you "the Russian."

Nikolai: Your pants...

Suzanna: Oh shit—I love these pants, just can't bring myself to throw them away. *(Pins her fly closed.)* There—better?

Nikolai: Oh...I didn't mind them the other way, ha... You are Maria's sister?

    Suzanna laughs.

Nikolai: What?

Suzanna: Yes. I'm Maria's sister... So, Nikolai, you want to help me roll this carpet? Maria's moving rooms or something.

Nikolai: She is moving her studio into this room?

Suzanna:	God knows why.
Nikolai:	The light in this room is much nicer.
Suzanna:	The light. Ah, of course. You're another painter, then?
Nikolai:	Oh, no. No, I'm not.
Suzanna:	That's refreshing.
Nikolai:	And you?
Suzanna:	God no. I hate art. There...it's rolled...we rolled it together. Wasn't that fun?

Enter Robert.

Robert:	Maria says to hurry because— Why hello, Nick. You here again? Who let you in?
Nikolai:	Paulina. I have brought the painting.
Robert:	Oh, yeah...well, since you're here, you can help with the move, eh? We'll do the loveseat. I'll take the carpet.
Suzanna:	Oh, darn, I wanted to do it.

Exit Robert.

Suzanna:	So, if you're not an artist, what do you do?
Nikolai:	Many things. I like to help artists...any way I can.
Suzanna:	Sounds like fun.
Nikolai:	And what do you do?
Suzanna:	Nothing.
Nikolai:	Nothing?
Suzanna:	Fuck all. It's fun, too. I have a car.
Nikolai:	Sounds...fun... Well, I should...
Suzanna:	Yes?
Nikolai:	Go see if Maria needs help...show her the painting.

Suzanna: Right. See you around.

Nikolai: What?

Suzanna: See you...around...around here maybe...see you...

Nikolai: Oh yes, of course, ha. Yes... See you around...see you. (*Exit Nikolai.*)

Suzanna: I look like shit.

SCENE 6

> *Friday, October 13, 15h30. Studio/salon. Robert and Paulina, who strips flowered wallpaper off the wall.*

Robert: But don't kid yourself. It's difficult being the only man living among three women. And you're not only women, you're sisters. I always get the feeling that there's some sort of conspiracy going on. You three seem thick as thieves. Well, maybe not you. I always feel like I can talk to you, Paulina. I know it's been rough for you these last couple of months. That's why I think we can, you know..."buddies in bad times." And I just want to say that I'm glad you've come to live with us—I mean, I know you've been here a year, but I'm just...I've never told you that I'm glad...and I am...yes. Beautiful day, eh? For a Friday the thirteenth. Maybe after we're done here we can take a walk up over the mountain. What do you say?

Paulina: No, thank you.

Robert: You've always gone and done what you've wanted. You were never afraid to tell them all to go to hell. You married Jerry despite...and you refused to see your mother in the hospital. Now, that hurt some people, but you stuck to your guns... How is Jerry, anyway? Have you spoken to him lately? We never really saw things eye to eye, but I respect his opinions and I've never told him that.

> *Enter Suzanna.*

Suzanna: Are you expecting me to carry the loveseat in by myself? Maria is driving me mad—she wants it out of her little fucking studio, so can we do that before I commit murder? *(Exits.)*

Robert: Thanks, Paulina. Back in a sec. *(Exits.)*

Paulina: "Have you spoken to him lately? Have you?" No, I haven't. I'm trying to kill him. Why would you ask me that? Why? Stupid, stupid, stupid. No...no... But why did he ask me that? No, don't think. Just don't think. Just stop thinking. He lied to me. No, he didn't. He was a liar, yes, but he didn't lie to me. No, don't think. Anything else. It's warm again. Yes. And I cut the dahlias. See? Again. Dead again. Killed them. Cut for nothing. I have to cut you. His head is huge. Don't worry. Open wide. I'll cut you and put your blood in a vase...oh, no, don't. Don't think. Please don't. Please, please, please.

Robert and Suzanna enter with the loveseat.

Robert: Agh! My hand, my hand! No, wait—

Suzanna: Well, if you lift your fucking end up—

Robert: Wait—no—wait...ok...there.

Suzanna: Oh, what am I doing here? What the fuck am I doing here?

Robert: I hope I haven't damaged a ligament.

Suzanna: Oh, and you sold the chairs.

Robert: What chairs?

Suzanna: Daddy's leather chairs.

Robert: I sold them?

Suzanna: Yes. You and Maria. As soon as you moved here. You don't remember, but you sold them to a Greek guy with hairy hands.

Robert: They were your father's? *(Phone rings off.)* Well?

Suzanna: Yes, they were Daddy's.

Robert: No, are you going to get it?

Suzanna: Get what? The—what am I, a secretary?

Robert: It's going to be for you.

Suzanna: I had no idea you were psychic.

Robert: Are you going to get it?

Suzanna: You get it.

Robert: I'm not going to get it. It would be a waste of my time. It's for you.

Suzanna: I'm not getting it.

Maria: *(Off.)* Is someone going to get that?

Robert: Suzanna, it's always for you.

Suzanna: What horseshit. I'm tired. I've been hoisting furniture.

Robert: One couch. *(Exit Paulina for the phone.)* Thank you, Paulina. Anyway, I don't much see the point in our having an unlisted number if you're handing it out left and right, writing it on bathroom walls...I'm sorry.

Suzanna: What?

Robert: I'm being unnecessarily nasty.

Sux   What's wrong with you today? Why don't you go take a jog? Why don't you go find someone to buy this house?

Robert: We're not selling this house.

Sux   Why do you want to stay here?

Robert: Why do you want to sell?

            Enter Paulina.

Paulina: Robert.

Suzanna: There's no privacy, all the rooms are attached—

Robert: Not on your floor—

Suzanna: You have to walk through—if I want to go out right now, I have to walk through her fucking studio.

Robert: You have your own entrance—

Paulina: Robert.

Suzanna: Anyway, that's not—

Robert: A bathroom, a kitchenette—

Suzanna: That's not the point—

Robert: What is the point?

Paulina: Robert.

Suzanna: I don't want to fucking live with you!

Robert: We never see you—

Suzanna: I don't want a home—

Robert: It's not as if—

Suzanna: I don't want to live with you.

Paulina: Robert.

Robert: What do you want, Suzanna?

Suzanna: What do I want? What the fuck are you, a priest? What do I want? I want my money.

Robert: You know my offer.

Suzanna: Oh please, half a million—that's half my share of this house.

Robert: Not in a buyer's market.

Suzanna: Half. And you know it, you asshole.

Paulina: Robert.

Robert: Mutual consent. That's what the will says. Talk to your sisters.

Suzanna: And you don't influence her.

Robert: Talk to your sisters.

Suzanna: I'll talk to her when you fuck her, how about that?

Robert: I'm sorry.

Paulina: Robert.

Robert: Yes.

Paulina: It's for you.

Robert: What's for me?

Paulina: The phone.

Robert: That was hours ago! Who is it? *(Exits.)*

Paulina: Somebody.

Suzanna: Why do you want to stay here? Don't you just want to have
            the money? Am I crazy to want that? Is it because I'm not
            thirty yet? Am I going to go soft on my next birthday? *(Blows
            her nose in her bloodied hanky.)* So, I met this Nikolai guy. Pretty
            strange. Have you met him? Nikolai... "for a nickel I will..."
            Maria invited him to dinner Sunday.

SCENE 7

> *Saturday, October 14th, 1h30. Bedroom. Robert and Maria
> make love in the dark.*

Robert: Sorry...sorry...

Maria: What?...what?...

Robert: Sorry...

Maria: What?...what is it?...Robert? What's the matter?

Robert: Sorry...where were you?

Maria: What? Where was—

Robert: You weren't with me.

Maria: What?

Robert: You weren't—I was somebody else.

Maria: I...what?

Robert: I'm sorry, I'm sorry I can't be somebody else.

Maria: Robert—

Robert: You wish you were with somebody else.

Maria: Don't—

Robert: You weren't with me. I understand. I wouldn't be with me. I'm not all here. You'd have to be with somebody else just to be with me.

Maria: Stop it.

Robert: I'm sorry.

Maria: Stop it, please.

Robert: I'm sorry...sorry... Who are you?

Maria: Oh, Robert—

Robert: No, I don't know you. I'm sorry, I don't. What was your father like?

Maria: What?

Robert: Just tell me.

Maria: My father?

Robert: You've never told me about your father. I've never told you about mine. They're both dead—maybe they know each other now.

Maria: Turn on a light.

Robert: No. Please. No.

Maria: This is stupid. What is the matter with you?

Robert: I'm sorry. I don't know anything about you. Who did you love more, your mother or your father?

Maria: I've had enough.

Robert: Don't. Stay. Stay, please. When your parents died, how did you feel? If my mother dies, I'll feel terrible. I didn't feel terrible when my father died. I don't remember feeling anything. I don't remember.

Maria: Robert—

Robert: We have to have children, our own children. I never see my son. If we don't have children soon, I'll never know my grandchildren. I'll be dead. They won't have a granddad.

Maria: Robert—

Robert: Why can't I talk to you about this?

Maria: Of course you can talk to me, but I want to see you.

Robert: No.

Maria: Why can't you look at me? Why do you have to talk like this? Why do you have to talk at all? If you're feeling all this, why don't you just cry so I can hold you?

Robert: Cry?

Maria: Cry. Then I could hold you...then I...

Robert: I don't know what you're talking about. I don't know what I'm talking about...I'm sorry.

Maria: ...can I turn on a light now?

Robert: Why did you tell Suzanna we haven't been having sex?

Maria: I never said anything of the kind.Why? Did she—

Robert: You didn't?

Maria: What did she say?

Robert: She said...I've been busy, Maria.

Maria: All right.

Robert:	I know I haven't...I've been busy.
Maria:	It's all right.
Robert:	I'm sorry if you've felt neglected.
Maria:	You're not busy now.
Robert:	No...no, I'm not...I'm sorry... Am I driving you crazy?
Maria:	No.
Robert:	Are you sure?
Maria:	Robert.
Robert:	Say something.
Mar	Lie down. Let's go to sleep.
Robert:	And this damn stock market thing.
Maria:	Let's sleep.
Robert:	They phone you up in the middle of a beautiful day—
Maria:	Sh. Just go to sleep, please.
Robert:	I'm sorry, Maria...I'm sorry...

SCENE 8

Sunday, October 14, 22h30. Salon. Paulina sits on the floor reading and listening to Schubert. On the wall the painting from Scene 2.

Paulina: Purple and puffed. And his tongue was green. I saw it. I saw and I didn't recognize it. It was a sign. I should have known. I should have known.

Maria: *(Off.)* Go on in, Nikolai.

Nikolai: *(Off.)* You need no help?

Maria: *(Off.)* We're fine.

Robert laughs off.

Nikolai: *(Enters.)* Oh, hello...ah, Schubert... The dinner was delicious... I understand that you made it...you didn't want to join us?

Paulina: Could you turn off the music, please?

Nikolai: What? Certainly...so...

Paulina: Before my ex-husband and I got married, we decided to live together and the first apartment we visited was a four-and-a-half on Durocher. The landlord said the tenant hadn't been in all day so he let us in with his key. But the tenant was there. He'd hung himself in the bathroom.

Maria: *(Enters with tray of coffee and cognac.)* I think we have you to thank for a wonderful dinner—have a seat, Nikolai—it was fabulous. Why are you sitting on the floor?

Suzanna: *(Enters.)* Your husband is driving me mad.

Maria: If you have a problem, you deal with him.

Robert: *(Off.)* "Marezee doats 'n dozey doats, 'n liddle lamzy divey..."

Suzanna: The one night I decide to eat with you—

Maria: He's just had a bit too much wine.

Suzanna: What's up with him these days? It's like living with Mr. Dressup.

Nikolai: Who is Mr. Dressup?

Robert: *(Enters with a scotch.)* "A kiddledy divey doo, wooden you?"

Maria: Robert.

Robert: *(To the painting.)* Why hello, Nick, ha ha. Great supper, Paulina.

Suzanna: Yeah, it was great, Paulina.

Robert: Yes, indeedy-doo: "Marezee doats 'n dozey doats—" You know, Nick, this song sounds like gibberish, but actually it makes sense. It's "Mares eat oats and does eat oats"—you know, doe, "a deer, ha, a female deer," ha.

Maria: Robert.

Robert: And little lambs eat ivy—

Nikolai: Hello, Pushkin.

Maria: Robert, please.

Robert: What? My mother used to sing us that song. We would laugh
            and laugh.

Suzanna: I'll put something on.

Robert: No, let's make our own music.

Suzanna: Really, Bob, we don't want to hear you sing.

Robert: "When you are in the last bloody ditch, there is nothing left
            but to sing."

Maria: What are you talking about?

Robert: Paulina knows what I'm talking about, don't you? Eh?

Suzanna: What does anybody want to hear?

Robert: In the old days, before radio or even television—wait, did I
            get that wrong?

Maria: Put on something quiet.

Suzanna: Quiet?

Robert: Ha, yes—before television or even radio—

Maria: Well, we want to make sure we can talk over it.

Robert: That's how people—families—entertained each other.

Suzanna: You mean you want music that's quiet or you want the
            music played quietly?

Maria: Suzanna.

Robert: They would sing songs and...tell stories...

Suzanna: Why don't we ask our guest what he'd like to hear?

Nikolai: Whatever you want.

Suzanna: So, you want to dance or talk?

Maria: Dance?

Nikolai: I love to dance—

Suzanna: Me too. So, what—

Maria: We're not going to dance.

Paulina: Perhaps something for the background would be more ap-
               propriate to this evening.

Maria: Yes, put on something backgroundy, like—

Suzanna: I know what I'll put on.

Robert: So, Nick—

Maria: Is it backgroundy?

Suzanna: No, it's devil-worship music, Maria.

Nikolai: Ah...lovely music.

Suzanna: Yeah, it's great, eh?

Robert: So, Nick, your wife didn't want to come tonight?

Nikolai: Uh...no.

Suzanna: You're married? Well, that's interesting.

Maria: What's interesting about it?

Suzanna: You don't smell married.

Nikolai: What does marriage smell like?

Suzanna: Old books. Mould.

Robert: Do I smell like old books, then?

Suzanna: You smell like a turn-of-the-century dictionary, Bob.

Robert: One day you will too.

Suzanna: Only married men mould. Married women dry out like fruit in a bowl.

Robert: I see. You once brought a fellow to dinner here—what was his name?

Suzanna: I don't remember.

Robert: Short fellow, kind of heavy—

Suzanna: Oh, Paul.

Robert: That's it. What became of you and him?

Suzanna: Nothing became of us, Bob—he's gay.

Robert: Eh?

Suzanna: He's just a friend.

Robert: The little fat guy? With the bow tie?

Maria: Anyway, that's the last time I remember you having dinner with us, period. What's the occasion?

Robert: That little guy was a fag?

Maria: Robert.

Robert: Well, I hope we washed the dishes thoroughly that night, ha ha. I'm kidding.

Suzanna: So, it's about your wife.

Maria: What about her?

Suzanna: Is she a Russian?

Maria: She's a Canadian.

Suzanna: So, you met her here.

Maria: No, there.

Suzanna: What are you, his press secretary? Where were you married?

Nikolai: In the Soviet Union.

Maria: Then she came back and waited a year and a half for him to be allowed to come here.

Suzanna: And I had this vision of you two crawling under barbed wire to come to Canada.

Nikolai: I'm sorry. Nothing so romantic. More like strangers at Mirabel.

Suzanna: Do you still—

Robert: So, Nick, do you play tennis?

Nikolai: I haven't played in years. I used to play quite well.

Robert: I was trying to think of a sport that we might have in common, besides hockey. And then I remembered there's a lot of great Russian tennis players. We should have a game sometime.

Nikolai: Certainly. You'd have to lend me a raquet.

Robert: No problem.

Suzanna: So, do you still have family in Russia?

Nikolai: Yes.

Suzanna: Do you hear from them?

Nikolai: Oh, yes.

Maria: Communication is a lot easier now that everything is opening up.

Robert: Everything's not "opening up," Maria.

Nikolai: You will see. The Wall will come down within a year.

Robert: You think so? Christ, I hope not.

Maria: What do you mean?

Robert: We're headed for a recession already. The last thing we need is a stronger Germany in '92—

Maria: I think anything that knocks down walls, frees people, is good.

Suzanna: You want some coffee, Paulina?

Robert: That's great, that's—that's your typical naive position. Artists, eh?

Maria: How is it naive?

Robert: I'm not saying—of course, they should all be free, sure—tear down the Wall, etcetera. We just have to be careful.

Maria: So you think the walls should stay up.

Suzanna: *(Pouring cognac into Nikolai's cup.)* Having fun, Nikolai?

Robert: I think you don't know what you're talking about.

Maria: I hate these discussions of money as if they have nothing to do with people.

Robert: Right. Ok. I'm sorry.

Maria: We can't have any more of these repressive—

Paulina: We need communist countries. With no more communist countries everyone will want to buy all of the useless things we produce and we'll consume and consume until we drown in our own garbage. Then the Japanese will buy our garbage and turn it into quality footwear.

Robert: Ha ha ha, yes! You tell them, Paulina! Yes! Ha ha.

Suzanna: What time is it, anyway?

Nikolai: 10:30.

Robert: Well, darling, why don't we go to bed and let these nice people go home, ha.

Suzanna: That joke only works if the people don't live here, Bob. And Nikolai might as well be living here.

Robert: Well, darling? To the conjugal bed?

Maria: It's 10:30.

Robert: So it is. I have to get up early, see what the market is going to do...so, are you coming?

Maria:	Robert, it's 10:30.
Robert:	Right, right. No harm in asking, ha—excuse my glands. All right then, good night all. *(To Nikolai.)* Tennis, eh? *(Exits.)*
Suzanna:	Good night, Robert. Thank God. What's with him?
Maria:	I am not my husband's keeper. Oh, you were going to read me the thing.
Nikolai:	Which?
Maria:	The poem—
Nikolai:	Oh, yes—
Maria:	You said—
Nikolai:	It is unfinished—
Suzanna:	What's this?
Maria:	His wife's a writer—
Suzanna:	Oh yeah—
Maria:	And he told me he had a new poem of hers—
Nikolai:	As I said, it is a fragment—
Maria:	Oh, read it. I'm curious.
Nikolai:	She wrote this at— I found it this morning.
Suzanna:	You sure she wants it read?
Nikolai:	Let us say that she left it for me...
Suzanna:	Yeah, but does she want it read?
Nikolai:	It is mine. I do what I want with it.
Maria:	*(Turning music off.)* Do you want me to turn the music off?
Nikolai:	Oh...
Suzanna:	I can't believe we're reading poetry in the salon.

Maria: Tch.

Nikolai: *(Reads.)*
           "We live where it's cold
           where our words freeze mid-air
           between our mouths and ears
                   and hang there for us to see
                   little rags of words
           where we can't move for the frostbite that
           cracks pieces off us and lets them fall
           into the mouth of a huge dead soldier
           we can watch though—where we live
           silent still
           watching the shards of us fall
           into his mouth
           into his cold dead mouth
                   until our eyes break—"

           It is unfinished.

Maria: It's nice.

Suzanna: I don't get it.

Maria: Suzanna.

Suzanna: *(Turning music back on.)* No, seriously. I've never understood
           "art." You have something to say, but instead of saying it,
           you hint at it and then everyone applauds and goes out for
           drinks. Well, I can't be bothered trying to figure it out. Art is
           just avoiding the issue. If she's so miserable, why doesn't she
           just say, "I'm miserable"?

Nikolai: That wouldn't be very beautiful.

Suzanna: Ah, of course. Beauty. I've never understood that either.
           You'll have to explain it to me.

Maria: Oh, shut up.

Suzanna: What?

Maria: You don't understand beauty.

Suzanna: I mean I don't understand the attraction—

Maria: So how you dress is totally at random? Those blouses of yours?

Suzanna: Are you going to let me finish?

Maria: You sound like some nihilist teenager. You should tear up your clothes, stick pins in your face and bother people on streetcorners for change.

Suzanna: Can I finish? Never mind. I've got to go soon, anyway.

Maria: Does anybody really like this music? I don't mean in this room, I mean on the planet. (*Changes music.*) Have you seen the *Cents Jours* yet, Nikolai?

Nikolai: What? Uh, no, not yet—I was thinking of going this week.

Maria: Give me a call before you go. I heard it's not very good this year. They're in that new place on Notre Dame.

Nikolai: Yes.

Maria: I've never been a big fan of installations.

Suzanna: Well, this is a good time to exit.

Nikolai: Perhaps we should discuss a more common—

Suzanna: No, no, I've got to meet somebody, anyway. So good night. Good night, Paulina. (*Exits.*)

Nikolai: Good night.

Maria: Mmm...wasn't that wine wonderful? It's Algerian. Do you remember at the opening of Ludmilla's show? You gave me your red wine. I thought you were crazy, I thought "who is this guy?" Ha. Oh, you make me laugh...anyway...I'd like your advice on which watercolours I should select for my show. I'd show them to you now, but...you look tired. Also, I don't know, I'm not quite ready to show you them. Sometimes these things take time. Would you like some more coffee?

Nikolai: No, thank you... I...

Maria: I'm glad you came to dinner.

Nikolai: It was very therapeutic for me. I did not wish to say this at the table for reasons that are obvious, but Irina lost the baby yesterday.

Maria: What?

Nikolai: I am sorry if I have seemed a little distracted this evening. I have spent practically the last thirty-six hours at the hospital. It was too much. I had to get out.

Maria: It must have been awful. What happened?

Nikolai: I came home from getting the morning newspaper—the whole bed was covered in blood...just like that, she...it was horrible.

Maria: Is there a history of this in her family?

Nikolai: I don't know. She had complained of pains, but I never thought...there was so much blood.

Maria: How is she?

Nikolai: They're not sure. She must stay in the hospital for testing.

Maria: Actually, Paulina's an obstetrician—

Nikolai: I beg your pardon?

Maria: What does it sound like to you, Paulina?

Paulina: How many weeks was she?

Nikolai: Uh...seven or eight.

Paulina: There was heavy bleeding?

Nikolai: Yes.

Paulina: She had complained of abdominal pains?

Nikolai: On her left side mostly.

Paulina: Probably ectopic. Had she used an IUD?

Nikolai: Uh...yes...

Paulina: Poor thing. Have they removed the tube?

Nikolai:	I don't know.
Paulina:	Poor thing.
Nikolai:	She had complained of pain, but I thought it was normal to complain...it was horrible...
Maria:	I was wondering why you didn't return my calls.
Nikolai:	Yes, I hadn't the time until this morning—I didn't want to tell you over the phone—
Maria:	No, I understand.
Nikolai:	I should go home now.
Maria:	You must be exhausted...in an awful sort of way, you must feel relieved, though.
Nikolai:	I don't know.
Maria:	You can't hold yourself responsible for—
Suzanna:	*(Passing.)* Ok, then, 'bye.
Nikolai:	Wait, I am going too.
Suzanna:	Oh, you want a ride somewhere?
Nikolai:	Yes.

Exit Suzanna.

Maria:	Call me tomorrow? For the film Tuesday.
Nikolai:	Yes, Tuesday. Oh no, wait—I cannot on Tuesday. Wednesday?
Maria:	Ok.
Suzanna:	*(Off.)* I'm going.
Nikolai:	Yes, I'm coming. Thank you again. *(Kisses Maria on cheek.)* Good night.
Maria:	I'll walk you to the—
Nikolai:	No need. Good night. *(Exits.)*

Maria: Call me. Oh, I forgot to remind him about the *Cents Jours*... "We live where it's cold..."

Paulina: Could you turn the music off?

Maria: Hm? Oh, sure. *(She doesn't.)* Well, I'd better clean up.

Paulina: I'll do it.

Maria: You don't mind? I'm getting a headache all of a sudden. Thanks again for a lovely dinner. Good night, Paulina. *(Exits.)*

Paulina: Good night. No more. Not again. No. No more. No more lies. Lies. Lies. Lies.

SCENE 9

Wednesday, October 18th; 18h30—hospital room. Nikolai and his wife Irina (unseen); sound of a television news program. Lines in [brackets] are in Russian.

Nikolai: [I need to borrow some money...I need $400...do you have it?] I can pay you back next week. [Yes?]

Irina: In my purse...

Nikolai: You have—

Irina: No, the bank card.

Nikolai: I can pay you back next week. Fucking bank is trying to kill me, they won't...I can pay you next week—I have some money coming. What is your code?

Irina: What?

Nikolai: The code, the card code, the bank code.

Irina: I don't know...Anton.

Nikolai: Anton?

Irina: 2 - 6 - 8 - 6 - 6. A–N–T–O–N.

Nikolai: Anton...you don't need it?

Irina: What?

Nikolai: The money.

Irina: No.

Nikolai: I will—

Irina: Pay me back next week. You have some money coming.

Nikolai: If you don't want to give me the money—

Irina: I don't care about the money.

Nikolai: It's very cold out. It's snowing. You come home tomorrow. The doctor said I should come for you about noon. Are you going to say something? Am I here for a reason? I have to go soon.

Irina: Where are you going?

Nikolai: What good is it I stay here?

Irina: There's another hour of visiting.

Nikolai: Visiting, what visiting--there is no visiting, there is silence. (*To a patient off.*) Could you turn your television down, please? My wife...thank you. (*To Irina.*) A very ugly woman. The television doesn't bother you?

Irina: Where do you have to go?

Nikolai: I—where?...I'm meeting someone. We are seeing a film.

Irina: You're going to see a film.

Nikolai: This is crazy. [This is pointless. What am I doing here? How did my life become this joke?] What do you want from me? What?...We are finished Irina, we are dead. Enough. What kind of life could we have given a child? I am not afraid to say it: it is for the best that the baby died. It's for the best. I have to go.

Irina: I know what happened: the baby was punished.

Nikolai: It was not punished—

Irina: Sacrificed. We're dead, so it died. I know why you didn't die, you're everybody's friend. You help everyone. The world couldn't possibly lose someone as precious as you. So the baby was sacrificed.

Nikolai: Sh.

Irina: But why didn't I die? Why not me? I'm useless. Even my child didn't want to stay in my worthless body.

Nikolai: Irina—

Irina: There wasn't even a baby. I looked for it. There wasn't a baby. It was just blood.

Nikolai: I am going.

Irina: Why not me? Why didn't I die?

Nikolai: Stop it. You are not useless. No one was punished. It just happened. These things happen. There is no reason.

Irina: Why did you marry me? Why?

Nikola   I have to go.

Irina: To your film.

Nikolai: Irina—

Irina: With someone. Does this someone have a gender?

Nikolai: Irina, we are dead.

Irina: And if we went back to Moscow?

Nikolai: What?

Irina: You're right. You're here for no reason. No reason at all. I'll try to entertain you. Would you like me to start bleeding again?

Nikolai: [This is pointless.]

Irina: Stay.

Nikolai:	What is the point?
Irina:	I want you to sacrifice your film. I want you to sit here with me for an hour in silence knowing that you're missing a film.
Nikolai:	What would be the point?
Irina:	You owe me four hundred dollars.
Nikolai:	Good bye.
Irina:	Fuck you.
Nikolai:	I will come tororrow. *(Exits.)*
Irina:	You owe me four hundred dollars.

SCENE 10

Wednesday, October 18th; 19h00. Studio. Maria hums a song as she draws Paulina, who knits. Suzanna watches.

Suzanna:	Today's the day that Daddy died.
Maria:	Today?
Paulina	Yes.
Suzanna:	Eight years ago.
Maria:	Nikolai's been here eight years.
Suzanna:	*(Lighting a cigarette.)* You're quite smitten with this Russian, aren't you?
Maria:	Give me one.
Suzanna:	Maria!
Maria:	Just give me one.
Suzanna	Robert'll spank you.
Maria:	That would be something at least.
Suzanna:	Maria!

Maria:	Oh, fuck it. *(They laugh.)* And what did you say to him about our sex life?
Suzanna:	What? I didn't...well, maybe I made some joke.
Maria:	Well it hit home--but it's done me no good. *(Laughter.)* Seriously, what gave you the idea that we haven't been...
Suzanna:	I don't know...I looked at him. *(Laughter.)*
Maria:	Well, he wasn't always so...flaccid. *(Laughter.)*
Paulina	Sex is funny.
Suzanna:	Funny—you mean fun.
Paulina	No, funny. Sex is funny.
Suzanna:	You mean funny ha-ha or funny peculiar?
Paulina	Funny.
Suzanna:	Right... So what's with Robert these days, anyway? Besides his impotence, I mean.
Maria:	Suzanna.
Suzanna:	No, really. Lately he's been Mr...I don't know, Mr. Let's-Talk-About-Ourselves.
Maria:	Talk, talk...I don't know, he's...who knows what goes on in that mind of his. *(She hums to herself.)*
Suzanna:	It's nice that you're starting to wear some colors.
Maria:	You think?
Suzanna:	You used to look like you were in mourning. God, look at the snow.
Maria	Beautiful isn't it? I always loved the snow on the tree.
Suzanna:	Terrific—I have to drive in this.
Maria:	*(Maria hums.)* I hate that when a stupid song won't leave your head. Oh, did you see the ivy?
Suzanna:	The what?

Maria: At the side of the house. Somebody pulled bunch of it off of the wall.

Suzanna: Really?

Maria: Right at the side by the kitchen, a whole bunch of it. Did you see it, Paulina?

Paulina   Yes.

Maria: Must have been some kids.

Suzanna: Pretty weird kids. Why would anyone want to tear some ivy off a wall? So, you really are quite taken with this guy, aren't you?

Maria: You don't find him attractive?

Suzanna: Old Nikolai?..."for a nickel I will..." He's all right. In a quirky sort of way.

Maria: He...he says my name. He calls me Maria and it sounds...it sounds like he's talking about a woman—not "I'm sorry, Maria"...Maria...

Suzanna: "Say it soft and sounds like praying—"

Maria: Oh, fuck off—"Oh, Suzanna, oh don't you cry for me—" *(They laugh.)*

Paulina   There was never one for me.

Suzanna: No there was—we made it up, remember?

Maria: What?

Suzanna: Yeah, it was—it was...oh shit...you don't remember it?

Paulina   Not at all.

Suzanna: Yes, it was...oh, "Paulina the meana..."

Paulina   I was anything but mean.

Suzanna: No, Aunt Beth made it up with us, in New Hampshire.

Maria: What?

Suzanna: We were sitting in the dining room and Paulina said just that: "there's no song for me." So we made one up.

Maria: How do you remember this?

Suzanna: Oh, it was...agh! You don't remember?

Maria: Oh, don't move.

Suzanna: What?

Maria: Stay like that, both of you...

Suzanna: Oh, why can't I remember it? Anyway... So, if you like this Russian so much, why don't you do something about it? Does he like you?

Maria: He's here all the time.

Suzanna: That doesn't necessarily—no, I'm sure he likes you. So, do something.

Maria: Such as?

Suzanna: Has it been that long, Maria? You could always try—oh, I don't know—fucking him.

Maria: He's married. I'm married.

Suzanna: And in bliss, I might add.

Maria: Marriage has to have something to do with commitment. I mean—oh this damn pencil!—I'm married.

Suzanna: Well, his marriage is dull as death.

Maria: Why do you say that?

Suzanna: He needs a woman.

Maria: You can tell?

Suzanna: Maria, you're dying to fuck this guy.

Maria: Oh, god...I don't know.

Paulina   Fuck the Russian.

Maria: Paulina!

Paulina   Will sombody please fuck the Russian so that we can get on with life?

Maria: Oh, shit! This is no good. I don't know what's wrong with me, I hate everything I do these days.

Suzanna: The way I see it, this is the plan: dump Robert, sell the house and then run off to Moscow.

Maria: Oh, here we go—

Suzanna: Let yourself go for once in your life—

Maria: You're not the one to be telling me—

Suzanna: Do something—

Maria: To do something with my life.

Suzanna: I'm just saying—

Maria: You've said enough. Oh, by the way, someone keeps calling you.

Suzanna: Who?

Maria: He won't leave a name. He says he'll keep trying...

Suzanna: Look, the only reason you hang onto this house—

Maria: Suzanna, I don't want to discuss this.

Suzanna: The only reason you stay here is because of Robert.

Maria: What would you do with the money?

Suzanna: He's the one that—

Maria: Answer me that—what would you do? What do you want?

Suzanna: I don't have to justify—

Maria: You don't know what you want. You haven't a clue. You just want to make sure you have the money to buy "it"—whatever "it" is—if and when "it" comes along.

Suzanna: We're rich, Maria—

Maria: And you want to squander it. What about your children?

Suzanna: What?

Maria: When you'll have children—

Suzanna: I'm not having any children—

Maria: That's what you say now—

Suzanna: Where the fuck did these children come from all of the sudden? Who said anything about children?

Maria: You won't have anything left to give them.

Suzanna: Suddenly there's the patter of fucking little feet.

Maria: You treat life as if it was a shopping spree.

Suzanna: Thank you for explaining me to myself, Mother.

Maria: Well, I should get ready. I'm going out.

Suzanna: You never want to discuss this.

Maria: Oh Suzanna, what is the point?

Suzanna: You won't even consider my feelings in all this. What I might want. Right away you assume—

Maria: Two years you've been saying the same thing—

Suzanna: Right away you assume that what you want is more important than—

Maria: We already sold one of the houses—

Suzanna: Oh please—you just sold that one—

Maria: As soon as Mother died—

Suzanna: You just sold it because you and Robert already have a summer home—

Maria: And what did you do with the money then?

Suzanna:	Don't try and—
Maria:	What did you do with the money then?
Suzanna:	That is none of your business—
Maria:	Are you broke? Is that it?
Suzanna:	I have always wanted to sell this house—for two years now—
Maria:	You're broke, aren't you?
Suzanna:	From the moment she died, I said "sell it"—
Maria:	You might try working for your money—
Suzanna:	The money from this house belongs to me—
Maria:	Try doing some work—
Suzanna:	Why—work. You're always throwing this word at me.
Maria:	Well, you haven't done any since Mother died—
Suzanna	"Work, Suzanna, work"—
Maria:	You've just quit everything—at least when Mother was alive you—you went to school—
Suzanna:	Yeah, but what about what I want?
Maria:	Since she died you've been idle—lazy—
Suzanna:	What about what I want?
Maria:	You wouldn't be getting away with this if Mother—
Suzanna:	You have no right—
Maria:	If Mother was alive—
Suzanna:	So, what are you then, are you "filling in for Mother"? Are you "looking out for me" like she was? Who do you—you're my sister, ok? My sister. You have no right to think you're better than me because you're "married" or something—
Maria:	Why do I bother discussing—

Suzanna: To that impotent asshole—

Maria: Oh, that's enough—

Suzanna: What? You're "respectable"? You're, what? Better than me?

Maria: Just do some work—

Suzanna: I don't have to earn your respect—I'm not asking for my
           fucking allowance—that money is mine—

Maria: Work, Suzanna—

Suzanna: Work? Oh, like what you're doing right now? Are you
           "working" at this moment? We're rich, Maria. Let's not
           bullshit ourselves. We are rich people and let's act accord-
           ingly. I want that money—

Maria: Why? So you can piss it away in Europe instead of Montreal?

Suzanna: Paulina, isn't she just like Mother?

Maria: Leave her out of this—

Suzanna: You're the only one that ever stood up to her, that ever had
           the guts—I didn't, I admit it—I never had the guts to tell
           Mother to fuck off.

Maria: You never used to swear so much—

Suzanna: You did, Paulina—now tell her: isn't she just like Mother?

Maria: Why are you dragging Paulina—

Suzanna: I want her to tell you what a cunt Mother was—

Maria   Oh, that's enough—

Suzanna: She all but cuts André out of the will—

Maria: André is a lunatic—

Suzanna: There, you see?

Maria: André chose to go off and throw away—

Suzanna: Of course you understand her, you're just like her.

Maria: Mother has nothing to do with this—

Suzanna: You're as cold as she was--as frigid—

Maria: Just stop—

Suzanna: That was a cruel fucking hoax she pulled on us—

Maria: Will you stop—

Suzanna: Is this her way of forcing us to be a family?

Maria: Profaning—

Suzanna: There is no family—the house—

Maria: Mother has nothing—

Suzanna: The house is more important than the family—

Maria: You've done—

Suzanna: Than the people in it—

Maria: No.

Suzanna: Daddy never would have left us like this—

Maria: You—

Suzanna: Why did he have to die first? Why didn't she die?

Maria: Suzanna—

Suzanna: I'll never forgive her—I hope she's in hell—

Maria: Stop it—

Suzanna: I hope she's frying—I hope her skin is peeling off.

Maria: Shut up.

Suzanna: I do—I hope she's—

Maria: Shut up! I am not going to sell this house so that you can
              drink the money or fuck with the money or do whatever the
              hell it is you do with your excuse for a life. Is that clear?

Suzanna: It's my money.

Maria: Oh, you're impossible.

Suzanna: Some family.

Doorbell.

Maria: Oh damn it—what time is it? That's Nikolai...we're going to a film...oh, I'm a mess.

Suzanna: I'll let him in. *(Exits.)*

Maria: Would you? Oh, she's impossible...I was wondering why she was hanging around here tonight...I'm all upset...We're going to see a Polish film..."Film Bref Sur L'Amour"...ha...it's supposed to be very good...I'm like a schoolgirl, Paulina—I'm so nervous, I'm trembling. *(She puts her head in Paulina's lap.)* I'm like a schoolgirl...

SCENE 11

Monday, October 23rd; 10h15 Robert's sports club's locker room—Robert and Nikolai dress after a tennis match, Robert on a cellular phone.

Robert: It'd better be important, Steve...yeah... So what's the problem?...and?...well, what does he want? I don't understand...no...no, sign him—I've already got a buyer for the building...well, what?... You're kidding me. He cried? He...I can't believe...really?...no, it's not that, it's that I can't believe you're calling me up on my leisure time to tell me that a grown man cried in my office. Did his mother just die? No. He's just a lousy businessman, that's all... What? What loyalty? To whom am I being disloyal? He lost his businss, he owes the money, if anything, he's the—oh, look, enough: Steve, sign him—I want him signed by the time I get there, which will be in half an hour. I want him out of my office—no, no, wait, keep him there. I have a few words to say to him about loyalty. All right? Oh, and did Mulroney call yet? The bastard... All right—what? No, Steve... No, Steve—good bye, Steve. Sorry about that, Nick. I've got to stop carrying these things around. Where were we?

Nikolai: Have you heard of these erotic carwashes?

Robert: I beg your pardon?

Nikolai: Naked women that wash your car.

Robert: What, like in a burlesque show?

Nikolai: No, as you sit—

Robert: Oh, you mean you're in the car.

Nikolai: Of course. You drive in and—

Robert: These naked women soap your car and what-not... Are you allowed to get out of the car?

Nikolai: No.

Robert: Are they allowed in?

Nikolai: I don't think so.

Robert: So you just sit there in your car while these naked, tattooed women...I get it. Why are you telling me this?

Nikolai: As I was saying earlier: the freedom—

Robert: Oh, yes, the freedom, right—

Nikolai: We—

Robert: Always the large topics with you.

Nikolai: It is difficult for you here to understand what we—

Robert: Wait, but what do you end up saying with this freedom? Erotic carwashes? Pretty impressive. And these artists, Nick, some of the garbage—I mean, some of the things my wife has dragged me to...

Nikolai: In a free society we must allow for a certain...delinquency.

Robert: There's got to be limits, Nick. Some of these artists, I mean, they actually make money.

Nikolai: We must assume that eventually the audience will be intelligent enough to—

Robert: Ha, nobody ever went broke underestimating their audience, Nick.

Nikolai: The money is not the point. The audience's intelligence is not the point. The freedom to say anything—

Robert: But when you can say anything you want, everything ends up having the same value, right? Nothing is important.

Nikolai: The wrapping paper is as important as the present.

Robert: More important, Nick. And another result of your freedom: that painter friend of yours, we bought the—

Nikolai: Ludmilla.

Robert: Godawful thing, by the way—I love my wife too much. Anyway, you said yourself, she was good back home but now that she's "free" she paints dreck.

Nikolai: I would not say she paints dreck—

Robert: No resale, Nick, I promise you. Our Borduas, now that has resale, our Lemieux... Anyway, this freedom stuff is nonsense. It depends on what you want to talk about. I mean, look at Jerry—Paulina's ex. He's a Marxist, he was with some party—I don't know which, this was ten years ago—anyway, they still tap his phone. Oh, yes. He used to answer the phone, "Fuck the RCMP." I hated it when he called our house.

Nikolai: But he is not persecuted.

Robert: No... I mean, they let him teach at a CEGEP...

Nikolai: That is the difference... What is the matter with her?

Robert: Who, Paulina? Oh, she'll be all right. She's just going through some tough times.

Nikolai: But she is a doctor?

Robert: An obstetrician, yeah. Mind you, "for the people," eh? She worked for peanuts in one of those shelters: raped pregnant teenagers, stuff like that. She's a tough lady.

Nikolai: I do not see tough, I see—

Robert: Oh, don't count her out. She was never much of a talker anyway.

Nikolai: Where is my money!

Robert: What?

Nikolai: I had money—in an envelope. It's not here.

Robert: Hang on, now.

Nikolai: It was here. It—

Robert: I'm sure no one broke in—are you sure you had it with you?

Nikolai: Yes, I—oh, here it is...ha. It is not my money, it is my wife's.

Robert: Your wife, your wife, we keep hearing about this lady. Does she really exist?

Nikolai: *(A wallet photo.)* Here.

Robert: Wow. Is this recent? Nice-looking woman. What are you doing hanging around our house so much?

Nikolai: I was not made for fidelity. I love women too much for that. And I prefer the conquest...the hunt and the kill, to the actual eating of the beast.

Robert: Uh huh...who are you planning on killing at our house?

Nikolai: *(Stares at Robert a moment.)* No, no, ha... I am speaking in generalities.

Robert: Oh, you son of a bitch, ha.

Nikolai: And you? You find that you can be satisfied with just one woman?

Robert: I've spent a good deal of my time thinking about myself these days, Nick—you could almost say I've had a bit of a crisis lately, maybe you've heard something about it? The side effects? No? Anyway, there are a couple of things I've figured out: first, I'm a rich man. In a few years I'll be so rich that, without working, I'll keep getting richer. Second, there's nothing wrong with it. Nothing wrong with me. And then I started thinking about all the things I have, I already have everything. A few nice homes—I have a little house in Spain that even Maria doesn't know about. I have an ex-wife and a kid I never see. I have all of it. And the last thing I realized is that I love my wife. So this weekend is her birthday. I'll take her down to Stowe, spoil her a bit. Get us back on track.

Nikolai: "The best things in life are free."

Robert: No, they're not. Not in my world. Maybe in yours. What is your world, anyway?

Nikolai: How do you mean?

Robert: What do you do? For money.

Nikolai: Various things.

Robert: Guys like you fascinate me: I mean, why do I like you, Nick? I don't know how you did it, but you got to me as well. We all like you. But who are you? No one has the slightest idea. The only thing I know about you is that you're in debt. I smelled that right away. But it doesn't really matter, does it?

Nikolai: It's not that mysterious.

Robert: Yeah... Anyway, good game.

Nikolai: I was rusty.

Robert: Oh, you're damn good—you really had me going in the second set.

Nikolai: Perhaps next time I will win.

Robert: Maybe...can I drop you off someplace—ha, my house?

Nikolai: No, thank you...and how is Suzanna?

Robert: Suzanna? Rarely see her, you know. I tried to get to know her, but frankly, I think she hates me too much. After you. (*Exit Nikolai.*) Yup, she hates me, hates the air I breathe, ha. What can you do? Sisters, eh? Sisters, sisters, sisters.

SCENE 12

> *Thursday, October 26th, 22h. Phone room. Maria, in candle-*
> *light, on the phone. Shadow of Nikolai on the other end.*

Nikolai: Is anything the matter?

Maria: Nothing really...I just wanted to call...how's Irina?

Nikolai: She sleeps most of the time. I cannot take her anymore.

Maria: We're going away for the weekend.

Nikolai: Yes, you were telling me.

Maria: We leave tomorrow...it's my birthday Sunday.

Nikolai: Yes.

Maria: I asked Robert, we'll be home Sunday, late afternoon. Would you like to come for dinner?

Nikolai: Certainly.

Maria: Come around five...don't bring Irina.

Nikolai: I won't.

Maria: I don't mean—I mean, don't choose this time to bring her if that's ok.

Nikolai: I wouldn't.

Maria: I'm glad I caught you in...there's another fire at the home across the street.

Nikolai: Really?

Maria: The power's out again. I'm in the dark. I have a candle and I'm looking out the window. I can see my reflection and through my reflection there's the fire... Did you enjoy the show last night?

Nikolai: Oh, like I said: me and country music...

Maria: Right, right...I don't know why I called...I just wanted to hear your voice.

Nikolai: Well, here it is.

Maria: Ha, yes...

Nikolai: How is everyone?

Maria: Robert is out. Paulina is...the same. We hear her walking around in the dark... With the power out—are you still there?

Nikolai: Yes.

Maria: I can't really work...do you have power at your house?

Nikolai: *(To Irina.)* What? Just a minute. *(To Maria.)* Maria, she is awake. I must go.

Maria: Ok.

Nikolai: She is driving me mad. I can't breathe.

Maria: Please come—

Nikolai: *(To Irina.)* Yes, yes, just a minute! *(To Maria.)* I'm sorry.

Maria: Please come on Sunday.

Nikolai: Yes, at five.

Maria: I'll see you—

Nikolai: Yes, I'm sorry—goodbye. *(Hangs up.)*

Maria: Ok—Sunday...I'll see you Sunday...

SCENE 13

> *Sunday, October 29th, 16h40. Salon. Nikolai and Suzanna.*

Suzanna: Is that for Maria?

Nikolai: Of course.

Suzanna: The wrapping is cute.

Nikolai: It's so warm.

Suzanna: How's your wife?

Nikolai: She's fine.

Suzanna: She's home, then?

Nikolai: Oh, yes—what time is it?

Suzanna: You're early.

Nikolai: How—according to my watch—

Suzanna: Did you set it back?

Nikolai: Back?

Suzanna: Last night we set them back.

Nikolai: Oh, of course, ha.

Suzanna: Spring ahead, fall back.

Nikolai: So it is quarter to five, not...of course.

Suzanna: It's a good thing I was here. To let you in.

Nikolai: Where is Paulina?

Suzanna: Last I heard she was lying down. I heard her lying down. She lies down very loudly. I think it's all that cooking she does. You never bring your wife to dinner with you. She doesn't like to eat? Does she have a nice mouth?

Nikolai: A nice what?

Suzanna: Mouth. Her lips and tongue. You have a nice mouth. Do you like mine? I only ask because we watched each other eat all night once... Never mind. I'm just being silly. Is your wife the hypochondriac?

Nikolai: Not really.

Suzanna: Who's the one married to the hypochondriac? I get all the friends' wives mixed up.

Nikolai: I don't know.

Suzanna: Who's the one married to the woman who likes men from underprivileged countries?

Nikolai: I don't know all your sister's friends.

Suzanna: And who's the woman married to the real estate asshole who wants to fuck the Russian?

Nikolai: Are you sure she wants to...fuck him?

Suzanna: You almost couldn't say it. That's very funny. Say it. It's easy: fuck. Fuck, fuck, fuck. You know what it means? You put your thing in my thing and we move together. Say it. Say it like you spell it: fuck.

Nikolai: You shouldn't be so vulgar.

Suzanna: I shouldn't be so bored, so dead and trapped in this fucking house, that's what I shouldn't be.

Nikolai: Should we not turn on a light?

Suzanna: So, you're happily married then. (*She laughs.*)

Nikolai: What do you want?

Suzanna: Want?

Nikolai: Yes.

Suzanna: People are always asking me that. I never know what they mean... So, are we going to do this?

Nikolai: What?

Suzanna: Because they'll be home soon...are we?

Nikolai: Are we what?

Suzanna: Going to dance.

Nikolai: Dance.

Suzanna: You told me you loved to dance. I'll put on music.

Nikolai: You've lost me here.

Suzanna: Oh, no. No, I haven't. I've lost a lot of things, but I haven't lost you. You don't come here to see my sister anymore. So why do you come here? She wants you to fuck her and you're not going to fuck her. You're not interested. Because if you were interested, you'd have fucked her by now. This is a big house. It's very easy to fuck someone in this house. Lots of rooms. Why, this room even. *(She removes her panties from under her skirt.)* It is hot in here. *(He approaches her.)* No, don't kiss me. Don't. Just do it. *(They try to fuck standing up.)* No, wait. Wait. Here.

> *She bends over the loveseat. He takes her from behind. The room is dark. The door opens slowly. Paulina stands in the doorway with an axe. She walks slowly towards them...passes by them, exits. They do not notice her.*

Suzanna:　The door...it's...the door's open...the door's open...it's open...

> *It is finished.*

Suzanna:　*(Giving Nikolai the now-crushed present.)* Oops...

Nikolai:　Perhaps I should go.

Suzanna:　What? Why?

Nikolai:　Suzanna.

Suzanna:　How did the door get open? It was closed, wasn't it?

Nikolai:　I...

Suzanna:　What?

Nikolai:　No, nothing.

Suzanna:　No, what?

Nikolai:　It's nothing...I should leave.

Suzanna:　How did the door get open?

Nikolai:　I should go...

Suzanna:　Turn on a light. We should have used a condom, you know. You animal. You'll have to come visit my sister again sometime... What is it?

Nikolai:　I...

Maria: *(Off.)* We're home. Hello?

Suzanna: Turn on a light.

SCENE 14

Sunday, October 29, 17h00. Salon. Suzanna and Nikolai. Maria at the door. The phone rings off.

Maria: Would you get that, Suzanna?

Suzanna: Robert'll get it.

Maria: Robert went back out to get some things. Please.

Exit Suzanna waving her panties at Nikolai behind Maria.

Nikolai: Happy birthday. I brought you—uh—I dropped—

Maria: Thank you. Don't I get a kiss?

Nikolai: Of course. *(She offers her mouth, he pecks her cheeks.)*

Maria: You smell like perfume.

Nikolai: What? Oh, it must be...Irina—or perhaps, we were talking and...my watch, you see—I came too early because I forgot to change...how was the weekend?

Maria: I thought about you.

Nikolai: That is nice...

Maria: No, I mean, I thought only about you. I don't think anything else entered my mind.

Nikolai: I... *(Maria laughs.)* What?...what is funny?

Maria: You...you make me laugh. You're so beautiful. I want to laugh when I see you, you make me so happy. I haven't seen you in four days and now I see you and I'm so happy, I'll leave him. *(Falls to her knees.)* I can't believe I'm looking at you. I'll leave him. Seeing you here, I don't care. I'll dump him, I'll sell the house. I don't care where we live, we can live in a doghouse.

Nikolai: What are you doing?

Maria: I'm nothing—I'm a flake, a—I'm a dustbunny, ha. I love you.
             Say my name.

Nikolai: GET UP!

Maria: What?

Nikolai: Get up, now. Up.

Maria: What is it?

Nikolai: Get up. Don't. Get up.

Maria: Have I...I'm sorry...I...have I made a fool of myself?

             Enter Suzanna.

Suzanna: It's for you...you, Nikolai.

Nikolai: For me?

Suzanna: The phone. Some Russian guy. I had a hard time understand-
             ing him.

             Exit Nikolai.

Suzanna: You had good weather for your weekend.

Maria: Go away.

Suzanna: What?

Maria: Please leave me alone.

Suzanna: I have as much right to be in this room as you.

Maria: What?

Suzanna: You can't order me—

Maria: Just leave me alone. Please.

Suzanna: All I said was—

Maria: Please.

Suzanna: —you had nice weather for your trip.

Maria: You care?

Suzanna: Did he say something?

Maria: Who?

Suzanna: Nothing.

Maria: What are you talking about?

Suzanna: I'm not talking about anything. I—

Maria: Don't. Don't give me your small talk.

Suzanna: I was asking—

Maria: Shut up. You were "asking."

Suzanna: If you had a shitty weekend, don't—

Maria: How was your weekend?

Suzanna: What?

Maria: Did you wake up in time to see the sun at all? Or were you too busy fucking another stranger?

Suzanna: What's eating you?

Maria: What are you, anyway? You live in the dark. You vampire. You slut.

Suzanna: Why are you calling me that?

Maria: Shut up.

Suzanna: I asked if—

Maria: Why do you insist on talking? What gives you the idea that you have ever said anything of any importance?

Suzanna: Maria—

Maria: You have never uttered a word of any consequence in your life. They should remove your vocal cords. You're worthless.

Enter Nikolai.

Nikolai: I must go—

Maria:　　Yes.

Nikolai:　My wife...she tried to kill herself. What have I done?

Suzanna:　Shit.

Nikolai:　What have I been doing?

> *Enter Paulina covered in mud. She approaches Nikolai.*

Paulina:　I did it. I'm dirty. I did it. It was filthy, but I did it too. I fucked it. I did it.

SCENE 15

> *Monday, October 30th, 8h00. Kitchen. Robert on the phone.*

Robert:　Cancel it...No, something came up at home—what's my first available opening? All right, insist on that. Tell him, tell him what? I don't know. Find a good excuse—isn't that part of your job description?

> *Paulina enters, sits.*

Robert:　I'll be in lunch time the latest—and tell Steve to call me here as soon as he gets in—no, here, here at home. As soon as Steve gets in—that's right. Ok? Sorry to call so early, but it's a bit of an emergency. Fine. (*Hangs up.*) Did you see the tree? No, how could you see the tree, you just got up. Anyway, it's finished. Some maniac attacked it. I went out for my run and I saw—it's like someone took an axe or something and just hacked away at the, the, the roots, the trunk—it's all chopped up, the earth around it. It's dead—it can't be saved, I know it.

> *Exit Paulina.*

Robert:　Testa is coming right over—I woke him up—anyway, he'll be here and I promise you they'll have to cut it down. I don't know what's going on around here, but it's going to change. I take my wife on a weekend and she's a zombie. I leave the country early for this dinner—I go and get a cake, I come home and everybody's gone. No dinner. Nothing. I didn't eat. I made a sandwich. And my wife doesn't want to see me—locks herself in her studio...and now, the tree.

Re-enter Paulina with a pumpkin on a plate and a large knife—sits and begins to clean it.

Robert: No, but what the fuck is going on around here? No more. No more Mr. Nice Guy. No more.

Enter Maria.

Maria: Why are you shouting?

Robert: What are you doing up?

Maria: I couldn't sleep.

Robert: Poor you. The tree is finished.

Maria: The tree?

Robert: Some, some...drug addict attacked it. It's...it's—I promise you, it'll have to be cut down.

Maria: Oh, no.

Robert: "Oh, no." Oh, no. That's all you can say. The tree—it's two hundred years old—

Maria: Robert, I have a headache.

Robert: Then go back to bed.

Maria: Robert—

Robert: Don't! Don't "Robert" me. Artist! Don't. After this weekend, I think I have the right to a "Robert"-free month. All right? Artist? It's too early for you—go back to dreamland. All right?

A car honks outside.

Robert: That's Testa. If this tree is dead—if it's dead...I'll kill. *(Exits.)*

Maria: He's right...maybe I should go back to bed...did you make coffee?

Paulina: It'll be ready soon. *(Pause.)* I think I'm going to need a root canal.

Maria: A what?

           Enter Suzanna.

Suzanna: What's going on out there? *(Sees Maria.)* Don't start with me.

Maria: Don't what?

Suzanna: Don't start.

Maria: I didn't say anything.

Suzanna: Well, don't.

Maria: *(Crying.)* I can't...ok?...I won't...I can't...

Suzanna: What? What did I say?

Maria: I can't take it.

Suzanna: I didn't say anything.

Maria: I can't...

Suzanna: I'm sorry...stop crying...I'm sorry *(Crying.)* I'm sorry...don't... *(They hug.)*

Maria: I'm so miserable...I made such a fool of myself...

Suzanna: Maria...

Maria: I thought he liked me—I thought that was why he kept coming here—I made such a fool of myself...why should he like me? What's there to like?

Suzanna: Shh. It's ok. He's nothing. Believe me.

Maria: But why did he keep coming here?

           Paulina exits to turn on a radio. Re-enters and continues cleaning the pumpkin. Radio news plays quietly in the background.

Maria: I'm sorry...

Suzanna: No, I'm sorry...

Maria: What are you sorry about?

Suzanna: Oh, fuck, I don't know—life...I'm sorry about life.

Paulina: I'm sorry too—ha, "I'm sorry, I'm sorry," ha ha.

Enter Robert.

Robert: That's it. It's fucked. It's finished. It has to be cut down. Testa took one look at it and said: "Sorry." I can't believe it. I cannot fucking believe it. Did anybody call? What time is it? Eight fifteen. No, not yet. If anybody calls while I'm out there, call me in. I cannot believe it. *(Exits, re-enters.)* If I said anything to offend anyone, I'm sorry. *(Exits.)*

Suzanna: What was he talking about?

Maria: Where did you go last night?

Suzanna: Out...just out.

Maria: I'm so sorry—the things I said. I drove you away.

Suzanna: Forget it...what happened yesterday with—

Maria: I'd rather not talk about it.

Suzanna: Did he...say something to you?

Maria: Please. Let's forget him. Let's forget he exists. The things I said to you...

Suzanna: Forget it.

Maria: I don't know why I called you those things. I was upset. It was my birthday.

Suzanna: Let's just forget it.

Maria: I've been thinking: children. Maybe that's what's missing in my and Robert's life.

Suzanna: Maybe...maybe years from now, future generations will look back at us and laugh so hard they'll all die of a cerebral hemorrhage.

Paulina: Inconsequential. Inconsequential lies. Lives. Lie like a life...cut faces into things...don't stop and think about it. Just cut, cut, cut, cut, cut.

Suzanna: Paulina, are you all right?

Paulina: No, Suzanna, I'm not. Not at all.

            A thud on the window.

Maria: What was that?

Paulina: I'll see. I see everything. (*Exits.*)

Suzanna: I'm worried about her.

Maria: Poor thing, she must be so lonely.

            Outside, the sound of a chainsaw.

Maria: I guess they're starting to cut it.

Suzanna: Cut what?

Maria: The tree. It has to be cut down.

Suzanna: No. Really?

Maria: Yes... What kind of tree was it?

Suzanna: The tree?...it's...

            Paulina enters holding a dead crow.

Paulina: It was this. See? It's not just me. They're dying all by them-
            selves. It was flying and then it died and fell. By itself. Just
            like that. I didn't kill it. I didn't have to. It died. I didn't do it.
            Not me. Not me.

            Outside, the chainsaw wails. There is a knife in the pumpkin.
            Paulina lays the crow on the telephone. The telephone rings.

                        The End

Anton. Susan Glover as Suzanna, Pauline Little as Paulina, Robert Higden as Robert, Maria Bircher as Maria, and Roch Lafortune as Nikolai

the rabbit stares at the man

NO CYCLE

A CYCLE OF FIVE STORIES
AFTER THE CLASSIC NOH THEATRE OF JAPAN

ABOUT THE JAPANESE NOH

The Noh is an aristocratic art form that dates back to the fifteenth century. The event is performed in cycles of five plays, each of a specific type. First is the God Play, or rising sun play, dealing with a deity. Second is the Warrior/History Play that tells the story of a famous battle. The Women Play celebrates the virtue of a woman. Then there is a miscellaneous group, of which the most common is the Madwoman Play, usually about a woman crossed in love. The final group is the Auspices Play, which again deals with a deity to complete the cycle. Between each Noh, a Kyogen—a short farce—is performed. An entire Noh cycle can take up to a day to perform.

The dramatic action of each Noh is virtually the same; the Waki (or listener, usually a wandering priest) meets the Sh'té (protagonist). The Sh'té is usually a ghost who is trapped on earth in another body. Through the Waki's questions, the Sh'té is transformed into his or her former self and recounts the events (religious, historical, amorous...) that have locked him or her to the earth. The telling of the story releases the spirit who is now able to ascend to heaven.

There is also a chorus of Buddhist observers who may chant narrative information or pertinent Buddhist scriptures. Musicians punctuate the action. There are also occasional "extra" parts, mostly used for narrative purposes. The chorus and musicians sit in the upstage left corner of the playing area and the Waki has a place extreme downstage left for when the Sh'té finally begins to tell the tale.

No Cycle is for five performers, each taking a turn as Sh'té in one of the five stories. Thus, in *Rabbit*, the Sh'té is the man and the Waki is the rabbit. In *Six Little Dreams*, the Sh'té is the dreamer and her counterpart, the dying woman, is the Waki. In *Still*, the blind woman who loses her tooth "becomes" Viv as the Sh'té and Lily is the Waki. The seagull is the Waki and the dancer the Sh'té in *Seagull/Her*. And finally, the husband is Sh'té to the chorus/Waki of the rest of the cast huddled around the scrawny Christmas tree in *And*.

I have used the structures of a highly religious drama to talk about my time as I see it, a time of spiritual poverty—no rebirth, no cycles— where the death and resurrection of Christ is celebrated with a bunny hiding chocolate eggs around your house.

— Harry Standjofski

THE PLAYS

1. *Rabbit* (God play)
   Easter

2. *Six Little Dreams* (Warrior/History play)
   Remembrance Day

3. *Still* (Women play)
   Father's Day

4. *Seagull/Her* (Madwoman play)
   Valentine's Day

5. *And* (Auspices play)
   Christmas Eve

THE KYOGEN

For this cycle of plays, the Kyogen function as scenery changes between stories. The changes are performed, with efficient clumsiness, by Player #5 (although others may help if necessary). Each Kyogen is performed to Elvis Presley's song "Love Me."

THE PERFORMERS

The play is for five performers. Players #1 and #5 are men, #2, #3 and #4 are women.

THE SETTING

A bare stage with wings on either side. A white back wall. Painted on the SL corner of the wall is the skeleton of a burned pine tree. From the ceiling above the audience hang many torn and bent black umbrellas.

As the audience enters, a slide is projected on the back wall. It reads:

> let me hear you
> sighing
> even though I know
> you're lying

PRE-SHOW MUSIC

A simultaneous mix of a Japanese Noh performance and Elvis Presley's earliest gold record hits.

No Cycle was first presented in Montreal by the Association of Producing Artists at the Théatre Elysée in December 1987 with the following cast:

Robert Higden (#1)
Louise Standjofski (#2)
Maria Bircher (#3)
Florence Figols (#4)
Harry Standjofski (#5)

RABBIT

The man	Robert Higden
His mother, the child	Louise Standjofski
His wife, first woman	Maria Bircher
Rabbit, nun, second woman	Florence Figols
Short man	Harry Standjofski

SIX LITTLE DREAMS

Dying woman	Maria Bircher
Dreamer	Louise Standjofski

STILL

Lily	Florence Figols
Blind woman	Louise Standjofski
Viv	Maria Bircher

SEAGULL/HER

Seagull	Harry Standjofski
Her	Florence Figols

AND

The husband	Harry Standjofski

Director	Harry Standjofski
Set and lighting design	Ken Gregg
Costumes	Ana Cappelluto
Stage manager	Ana Cappelluto

No Cycle was workshopped at Playwright's Workshop Montreal in 1986 and again in 1987. Michael Springate was the dramaturge. Thanks to Michael Springate, Catherine Cahill and Don Dunbar.

RABBIT

STATION 1—JUDGEMENT

7h29

The last minute of a dream before the morning alarm. Projected black and white film: hands washing themselves in a white water basin.

Actors onstage within the film light. The man (#1) dreaming, stands USC, back to audience. His mother (#2), in a black shawl, stands behind the chair crying silently, staring at an alarm clock. His wife (#3) sits on the chair facing front, eyes dead. Her left palm out to the audience, fingertips up, she repeatedly traces a cross on her left wrist, silently mouthing the words: "across for the hospital, down for the morgue." A couple (#4 and #5) perform a dance of incommunicability. After exactly one minute of silence, an alarm clock rings.

Blackout.

STATION 2—RECEIVING THE CROSS

7h50

The alarm stops—very dim light. The man stands facing the audience as though into his bathroom mirror, slowly brings a washcloth to his face. Over this action, a radio plays.

Radio: "...you ain't nothing but a hound dog,
cryin' all the time,
well you ain't never caught a rabbit
and you ain't no friend of mine." *(Song ends.)*

— Yes, and that was the King and one of his first hits, "Hound Dog." Ten minutes before news time here at CFUK. If you're driving in from the West Island...well, I suggest you stay home. I've never caught a rabbit. Have you, Dr. Bill?

— Can't say that I have.

— Then I guess we couldn't have been Elvis' friend either.

— One that certainly looks friendly is today's weather: another beautiful day—

— Spring is sprung—

— But hold on...a chance of snow this evening.

— Not snow.

The man's wife passes hurriedly behind him from USR. She has forgotten something, turns and exits from where she came.

Radio: — Mm, hm, the temperature will drop as a low pressure system moves into our area—

Wife: *(Exiting, simultaneously with "area—")* Shit.

Blackout.

STATION 3—THE FIRST FALL

9h15

The man stands CS staring across a vacant city lot. He wears a black trenchcoat, a cap, and carries a briefcase. Five seconds of him staring out.

One by one the other members of the cast pass and, seeing the man, stop and try to see what he is looking at. Finally, all five stare out at the audience for a few seconds. Then, one by one, they get fed up and exit, leaving the man, oblivious to all this, staring out alone again.

A rabbit (#4) enters from SR and come to DSL of man.

Rabbit: *(Presents self to audience.)* Rabbit.

                Rabbit kneels, back to audience, DSL of man, stares at him. The man sees rabbit, smiles slightly, becomes unnerved.

Man: Shoo. *(No reaction.)* Shoo...shoo!...shoo! *(Stamps his foot until scene's end.)* Skoo! Yah!... Boo!...damn rabbits. Shoo!... Sʜᴏᴏ! *(Stamps foot again—no reaction.)* BOO! Sh— Scram...shoo ...shoo...*(He smiles a loser's smile.)* Ok...ok...

                Man exits slowly SR. Rabbit watches him leave.

                Blackout.

STATION 4—MEETING MARY

                9h55

                The man's mother (#2), in a wheelchair, before a TV set extreme DSL. Television light only light. The man enters from USR, walks slowly to behind his mother, who does not notice him. He leans down and kisses her cheek. She starts slightly, sees him, smiles and extends a hand.

Mother: Fine, fine, how are you?

Man: *(Giving her an envelope.)* Fine.

Mother: What? What's this?

Man: It's a present.

Mother: *(Looking inside the envelope.)* What?

Man: *(Kneels by her.)* It's a present.

Mother: This is money. Why are you giving me money?

Man: Mom...it's dark in here. Want me to raise the blinds?

Mother: No. Ha. I thought you were the nurse. I thought the nurse had kissed me. I thought, "Oh my god." Ha. How's Cathy?

Man: She's good...busy.

Mother: What?

Man: Where's your furniture?

Mother: Downstairs. We put it all downstairs.

            They watch television.

Mother: We could have a garage sale.

Man: What is this you're watching?

Mother: What? Television. They're cooking a rabbit.

            *A clock chimes ten. He looks at his watch. His hand trembles
            slightly.*

Man: Your clock is fast. I have to go.

Mother: What? *(He kisses her.)* So soon? I never see you.

            *They smile at each other. He goes to USR; she watches televi-
            sion. He stops a moment and watches her.*

Man: *(Exiting.)* Bye, mom.

Mother: What?

            Blackout.

STATION 5—SIMON HELPS CARRY THE CROSS

            10h17

            *A bank. A huge rabbit cut-out holding an Easter egg. On the
            egg is written:*

                        an easter nest egg
                        ask about our RRSPs

            *The man enters slowly from USR looking at his bankbook, not
            noticing the rabbit. He stands in front of it facing out. There are
            no available tellers. He waits. Sounds of a bank. He feels some-
            thing, turns slowly and sees the rabbit. He stands, back to
            audience and stares at the rabbit which stares at him. His hand
            trembles slight. A nun (#4) enters from SL counting a wad of
            money. She stops—there seems to be a problem with the
            amount. She recounts and then, satisfied, exits SR. On her
            exit, a voice:*

Teller:	*(Off.)* Suivant, s'il vous plaît... Next?

> *The man turns and sees the waiting teller, gives a final glance to the rabbit and then comes to DC and extends his bankbook to the audience as though to a teller.*

Man:	I'd like to close my account.

> *Blackout.*

STATION 6—VERONICA'S VEIL

> *12h40*

> *The man stands on the street next to another man (#5) who is chewing on a black plastic coffee stir stick. They face out as though watching the remains of a traffic accident cleared before them. A voice is heard from off:*

Woman:	*(Off.)* VERONIQUE! VERONIQUE! VIENS-ICIT-LA! M'A-T CRISSER UNE CLAQUE A FACE! [GET OVER HERE! I'LL SMACK YOUR FACE!]
Short Man:	*(To man.)* Tu l'as-tu vu? 'Sti, c'tait 'coeurant. Moi j'tais jusse en face-la pis poume! Juste devant moi. Eh sacrement. *(The two men stare at each other.)* Do you see it?
Man:	No.
Short Man:	Oh, it was crazy tabernacle—they go skree-poume! Poor guy. Scrap his...fuck, BMW for some lady in a...Rabbit. It's good there was no one there, they go schoom, the... the...momentum, tsé? Do you see the guy? The ambulance? He finish—his face, no face, hostie. There was just...blood. You see there the...crisse...craques-la. The window. The blood. Viarge. He go *(Brings a hand slowly to his face.)* poume! Caulisse. The lady in the Rabbit, she had nothing—ben, her car is fuck, but she had the belt. She was hystérique ha wananana... Calvaire... You cold, man?
Man:	No.
Short Man:	Ben, you are shake.
Man:	I'm not cold. It's warm out.
Short Man:	Cold nothing to be sorry—

Man: I'm not cold.

Short Man: Ok...

> *Short man stares at the man, who smiles limply out.*

> *Blackout. In the black, sound of a single church bell.*

STATION 7—THE SECOND FALL

> *Very dim light. The bell contines to toll slowly. The man slightly DSC stands in silhouette looking at his watch. His mother is seated on a bench USL in her black shawl, staring again at her alarm clock. As the man speaks, the rabbit (#4) enters slowly from SL to just USR of the man.*

Man: Half way there. The park is full of kids because it's a beautiful day and somebody's dead...

Rabbit: *(Whispers to the audience.)* Rabbit.

Man: ...I hear the bell.

> *The rabbit turns and kneels, facing upstage behind the man. The mother puts down the clock and sings gently to the audience, accompanying herself with gestures.*

Mother: In a house within a wood
a little man by the window stood
saw a rabbit running by
knocking at his door

help me, help me, the rabbit said
or the hunter will shoot me dead
come, little rabbit, come with me
happy we will be.

> *The mother smiles warmly at the audience. The rabbit continues to stare upstage. The man faces out, a silhouette.*

Man: Somebody's dead...or somebody's married.

> *Blackout.*

> *Church bell stops.*

STATION 8—THE WOMEN OF JERUSALEM

14h15

A park. The man sits on a park bench watching a little girl (#2) draw on the ground with chalk. Behind them, two women (#3 and #4) pass from USR to USL pushing a stroller.

1st Woman: *(To 2nd woman.)* But nothing was said, that's what drove me crazy. Everyone just tried to ignore it. *(They exit.)*

Man: What is that you're drawing? Hm? What are you drawing?...You can tell me. It's very nice...what is it? You can tell me. What—

Girl: It's bunnies.

Man: Really. Why's he like that? Him.

Girl: He's sick. He's old and in bed. And this is his family, they're coming to visit him. They're bringing him eggs.

Man: You look like my mother. Why are you drawing ra—uh, bunnies? Did you see one? What's wrong? Is something wrong?

Girl: Where's my mom? Where's my mom?

Man: What? Who is she?

Girl: Where's my mom?

Man: Shh, she's here, she's somewhere, shh. I have to go.

The two women with the stroller re-enter from USR.

1st Woman: Nobody says anything—what's going on here?

Girl: MOM? MAAAAA... *(She screams until the scene's end.)*

1st Woman: What's going on here?

Man: Nothing. We were talking and he realized he's lost his mother—do you know him?

1st Woman: No. Who are you?

2nd Woman: *(To girl.)* T'as perdu ta maman?

Man: I have to go.

1st Woman: Where are you going? What's going on here?

2nd Woman: Tu parle-tu français?

1st Woman: Where's her mother?

Man: I don't know.

1st Woman: What did you do to her?

Man: Nothing. I have to go.

2nd Woman: Qu'est ce qui se passe? C'est qui lui?

Man: I have to go. *(Exits USR.)*

1st Woman: He's a sickie, I think. I think he's a sickie. Do you know her?

2nd Woman: Non. Elle est ou ta maman?

1st Woman: He was a sickie. I can't believe it. Look, he's running. Come back here!

2nd Woman: C'est quoi ton nom?

1st Woman: *(Exiting SL with stroller.)* Excuse me, do you know this little girl?

2nd Woman: Ok-la. De quoi est-ce qu'elle a de l'air ta maman?

Girl: Maaaaaaaaaaaaaaa...

        Blackout and silence.

STATION 9—THE THIRD FALL

    19h15

    The man's home. The bench against the wall USL. His wife (#3) stands facing front holding a small can of tomato juice, a bucket of water and a rag. The ends of the kerchief in her hair look like rabbit ears. She slowly pours the juice over the chalk bunnies on the floor, looks down at the mess.

Wife: Damn.

            *She kneels and begins to clean. The man enters slowly from
            USR, stands behind her.*

Wife: I spilled some juice. You didn't go to work today.

Man: No.

Wife: You have a bunch of messages on the machine. Mostly the
            office wondering where you were. And your sister called.
            Anyway, I didn't erase them.

Man: I paid all the bills today.

Wife: All of them?

Man: Everything. Next month's mortgage. The joint account is
            balanced.

Wife: Great... Your mother called just as I got in—she said you'd
            visited her this morning? Anyway, she talked and talked,
            believe it or not, something about money. She really wants
            you to call her.

            *The man kneels behind her and holds her hips as though taking
            her from behind. She laughs slightly.*

Man: What?

Wife: What are you doing?

            After a moment he sits and removes his cap.

Man: I saw a dirty movie today. Three actually. They were very
            funny.

            *She throws the rag into the bucket and sits next to him. She
            wants to say something. She doesn't say it. Very long pause.
            He notices her rabbit ears. Her hands are sticky. She rises and
            exits with the bucket.*

Wife: *(Exiting.)* I waited supper for you. We're having lamb.

            *As she speaks from off, the man trembles violently, controls
            himself, takes out his wallet, counts his money and then leaves*

> *the wallet on the bench, gives the room a final look and exits USR.*

Wife: *(Off.)* It's supposed to snow again. Damn winter drags on forever. I hate March. Maybe...maybe you'll feel better when the winter's over. I don't know what to say. I can't look at you and talk to you at the same time anymore. I spoke to your sister about you the other day—I hate doing that. Everybody's noticed it...everybody... I wish you'd say something. Are you going to call your mother? Are you hungry?

> *Blackout.*

STATION 10—STRIPPED OF GARMENTS

> *19h30*

> *Words projected on the back wall. The slide reads:*

> 19h30 it's snowing
> he walks to church
> almost easter and
> the church basement is
> full of people buying
> other people's old
> clothes

> *The man removes his clothes within the projected words.*

> *Blackout.*

STATION 11—ASCENT OF THE CROSS

> *Seven slides—seven last words.The man moves and speaks within the projected words.*

Slides:
he walks among the
bargain hunters and a fat
man steps on his foot

no one sees him slip
up a dark stairway past the
three rusty coatpegs

alone in the dark
chapel he's looking up at
the weeping virgin

the ceiling creaks and
the streelamps set the stained glass
glowing dim and cold

altar candles out
christ smells of old rainy wood
the cups are empty

kneeling by a pew
where the loaded pistol sits
heavy in his hands

he stands church centre
looking at Christ the barrel
is cold on his ear

The man:
(To the fat man.) Agh!
It's ok.
It's nothing.

(Sings.) "Where has the time
all gone to?/ Haven't done
half the things we want to/ Oh
well/ We'll catch up some
other time"

Hi, mom, it's me.
"What?" ha ha
...sorry...

It's cold in here

I do.
I do ha.
What's there to drink?

(Holding the gun.) Never let it
be said I never gave you
anything.
Never let it be said.

It's over. It's done.
There's a fly in here.
Waiter, ha.
(Slowly puts the gun to his ear.)
A fly.

Blackout.

STATION 12—DEATH

*Darkness and silence. After a moment, a gunshot, a spark on
the stage. Silence. The opening bars of Bach's "Mass in B
Minor."*

STATION 13—DESCENT OF THE CROSS

*The mass continues. Words projected on the wall. The man
silently moves within the words in slow motion.*

Slides: *The man:*
Something white has startled him   *The gun pointing above his head—*
he's shot a hole in the ceiling   *dazed he looks out. His eyes focus on*
it's snowing in the church   *something in front of him.*

a rabbit stares at him   *Man sees the rabbit—incredulous, he*
from the altar he shoots   *screams silently and shoots at it.*
and wrecks the chalice

rabbit running   *Man follows the rabbit with his eyes*
man shoots   *and, screaming silent obscenities,*
the virgin explodes   *aims and shoots.*

rabbit running   *Eyes wild, screaming and searching.*
snow in the church   *Spots it. Shoots.*
the dead's candles shatter

rabbit running   *Still searching—he has a hunch—*
the bullet tears   *whirls about and shoots.*
Christ's side

rabbit on the altar   *Searches again. Sees the audience as*
snowing in the church   *rabbit smiles, aims, shoots.*
Christ shot off his cross

no more bullets   *Missed. Tries to shoot again—*
snow swirling round the glass   *realizes that the gun is empty,*
blood sirens screaming   *realizes that he can't kill himself—*
church falling   *puts gun to his temple. Click.*
the rabbit stares
at the man

the rabbit stares at the man   *He backs to the wall, half laughing,*
                                         half weeping. At the seventh repeti-
This slide repeats seven times. Each   *tion of the slide he falls to the floor.*
time the words get larger, until they *Music and lights die abruptly.*
are just large black shapes around the
man.

STATION 14—BURIAL AND RESURRECTION

No one on stage. Blood runs down the wall. Words projected:

the man is dead

the church heard nothing there is

no rabbit

ha ha ha

SIX LITTLE DREAMS

for Aunt Lucy

Extreme DSL: a small white globe lamp. It underlights a dying woman propped up by a white pillow and covered to her neck with a red blanket. The globe remains lit throughout the piece.

Music fades in. From USR the Dreamer enters in silhouette. She is barefoot and wears a red dress with a black poppy over her heart. She carries a chair on which hangs a closed black umbrella. She places the chair centre and tries to open the umbrella. She can't. She sits and the two women look at each other. The Dreamer lights a cigarette and the dying woman closes her eyes. The lights warm on the Dreamer as the music fades.

Dreamer: I am alone. I am heavy. I am a blimp. A dirigible. Floating over an anthill. The siren wails and the ants scurry in my shadow. Water pours from me, from the holes in my legs. The ants think it's raining but it's me. The ants are white. I have never seen white ants. My legs touch down on the anthill and the ants attack but they are washed away by the water pouring from my legs. The siren wails, the ants attack and drown, attack and drown, and I think I'm falling. My shadow is getting smaller. The scattering ants make a word, a white word in my shadow. I almost understand it—and I'm awake.

The music fades back in and the lights dim on the Dreamer. The dying woman opens her eyes and watches as the Dreamer tries and fails to open the umbrella. The silhouette of a man crosses from USR to off USL, sweeping the floor. The Dreamer picks up her cigarette and the dying woman closes her eyes. The music fades as the lights warm again on the Dreamer.

Dreamer: The clock. The minute of silence. My students standing by
            their chairs watching the second hand. Sh. And when the
            minute of silence is up we will have to sing and I hate it, I hate
            it, I am fucking dreading it. We watch the clock. They're
            being good. How do I get out of here? I don't want to sing.
            Outside it wants to rain and there's a man at the back of the
            room a little man. The kids don't notice him. They're too
            busy watching the clock. And the little man is behind me. He
            chases away the crow that was on my shoulder; he's my new
            crow, a little dirty man, and he whispers to me: "Thirty more
            seconds and then you'll sing. The kids don't know what the
            songs are about but that's never stopped us before. Look:
            fifteen seconds."

            He laugh-whispers. The kids watch the clock. No. "We
            didn't know what the words meant either. And it didn't kill
            us. Look how well we turned out, hahaha." And the minute
            is up. Fuck. The kids look at me. I must lead them in song. No.
            There's a rumbling outside, like thunder or distant explo-
            sions or... The kids are staring at me. We must begin. No. I
            open my mouth. They take a deep breath—

            *The music fades in and the lights dim on the Dreamer. The
            dying woman opens her eyes slightly and a hand holding a
            damp washcloth appears over her head. Her face is wiped
            gently and the hand disappears. She closes her eyes, the music
            fades and the lights warm again on the Dreamer.*

Dreamer: On Nuns' Island, the nuns grazing peacefully, protected by
            conservation laws, hazy fields of nuns. And there behind the
            fence is the crashed airplane, where they keep God. I hide
            unseen in a bush behind the fence, trying to catch a glimpse
            of God. I think I see him, something is moving in the crashed
            plane shadows but I'm not sure. There's a boy in the bush.
            He's sweating a little and smiling at me. He's eating straw-
            berries. He leads me by the hand, sneaks me into the barn
            into a haystack. The nuns start sniffing around the stack—
            sniff sniff—and we giggle, holding each other tight. Sh. And
            he takes a strawberry and passes it from his mouth to mine.
            There's juice running between our mouths. The nuns start
            sniffing furiously and then they start dropping like flies, they
            make a little sound—ek—and then fall into the down...and
            my lungs are full of lead.

> *The music fades in and the lights dim on the Dreamer as she puts out her cigarette. The dying woman opens her eyes. A hand appears over her head again, holding a glass of water. The glass is brought to the dying woman's lips, she sips and the glass is slowly withdrawn. The music fades as she closes her eyes and lights warm on the Dreamer.*

Dreamer: I'm staring at my mother's door, my face at the doorknob. I look funny. Mom is through there but they won't let me in. Out the window down the hall I see that it's ready to rain. There's a white rat at my feet. It scurries to the stairway. An old woman in a shawl is puffing up the stairs. Her face is sweaty.

— Hi.

— Who are you?

— I'm your fairy godmother. Damn those stairs. So make your witch already.

— My what?

— Make a witch. Come on, I'm tired.

And I think, which wish? That's what she means. What wish?...To get through the door. To see Mom. She'll be pale, paler than the sheets, fading into the sheets, she'll be transparent, a little blood by her mouth, pale blood... I want them to let me in to see Mom—so I turn to my fairy godmother and she's asleep—

— Hm? What? Oh. Make a witch.

— Say it properly.

— A wish.

And she's gone. Whose door is this? Is this Mom's room?... This is my room.

> *The Dreamer looks at the dying woman, who opens her eyes.*

Dreamer: It's mine.

> *The women continue to look at each other as the light fades on the Dreamer. A man and woman enter from DSL. They are dressed in black with red poppies over their hearts. They stand over the dying woman. In the dim light their faces are in shadow. They whisper quietly to each other as they look down at the dying woman. The Dreamer tries to open the umbrella again. It starts to open, but not quite. She hangs it on the back of the chair as the dying woman closes her eyes. The music fades out and the lights warm again on the Dreamer.*

Dreamer: When was the war? How is it that I don't remember the war? I see the aftermath, that it must have been terrible. So why can't I remember? I think I'm a crow. Yes. I think I'm flying. Yes. Over the ruined city, flying to the church, the scorched church. Yes. I perch on His shoulder; He's chalk white, the chapel a shambles. Mushrooms everywhere, everything covered in mushrooms. Drowned white rats and mushrooms in the holy dish. And look: at the foot of the cross, the little dirty man smiling up at me. He tips his hat and he's bald, little mushrooms growing out of his head. And it finally rains, little drops hissing as they hit the smouldering pews. And I look down at myself and I'm a clock. No, I'm not. I'm a moth. And when the rain hits me I dissolve because moths are made of dust. And the rain that has me, the drop of my dust runs slowly down the burned wood, past his chalk-white feet, past the mushrooms, and hits the ground. And it doesn't hurt anymore.

> *Different music fades in. The dying woman opens her eyes and looks at the Dreamer, who sits. The couple standing over the dying woman hug and cry quietly. The music continues quietly under as the Dreamer speaks.*

Dreamer: I'm in a jar. So tiny, I'm in a jar. In the shadow of a tree. An ash, blown leafless. And there are faces oustide my jar, large faces peering down at me. They look funny. And the rain makes little water scratches on my jar, while on a bough of the ash a little blonde girl hangs by her hair, smiling at me. And I'm surrounded in my jar by the letters and photographs of the world that I love. And the wind blows my door ajar and sends the leaves swirling around me. And I'm very

warm. And I've written a poem:
>it's remembrance day
>and nothing means anything
>five seven and five

From off USR a lamp comes on. The Dreamer feels it.

Dreamer: This is it. I'll slip away quietly. I love you all. Good night.

>*The music continues. The Dreamer reaches behind the chair
>and produces a green apple. She places it on the chair and looks
>at the dying woman. Lights fade on the Dreamer as she takes
>the umbrella from the back of the chair. She opens it in silhou-
>ette. The umbrella is torn and ragged. She raises it above her
>head and walks slowly towards the light source coming from
>USR. She exits and her shadow becomes huge, then quickly
>disappears. The couple standing over the dying woman hold
>each other and cry quietly. The light off USR dies. The music
>ends and the dying woman closes her eyes. The small globe
>goes out.*

STILL

Father's Day, 11h00, very hot and humid. A small bridge by the locks where boats pass. A railing about four feet high across the front of the stage. Sound of water lapping the sides and the occasional seagull.

Lily, a young woman (#4), leans on the railing extreme DSL. She wears a red blouse, white baggy cotton pants and sandals. She wears glasses and a black umbrella hangs on the railing by her right arm.

She has been diagnosed as having breast cancer. She stares at the water below her. Church bells in the distance. She smiles slightly.

Lily: Bonjour, Papa. C'est Lily. Ça va? Bonne fête des pères. [Hi, Daddy. It's me, Lily. How are you? Happy Father's Day.]

Her smile fades. She stares at the water and traces a hand over her left breast. She does not hear the tapping sound that approaches from off SR. A young blind woman (#2), cane tied to her wrist, taps on from SR. She is only recently blind. She wears a green and white cotton T-shirt, black tights, black sneakers, and dark glasses. She stops USC, feels with the cane to downstage. Lily has still not noticed her. The blind woman begins to walk downstage, trips and slams to the ground face first. Lily is jarred from her thoughts and looks at the blind woman, who rises slowly to her knees.

Woman: Shit. *(Blood runs from her mouth.)* Shit. *(She reaches into her mouth, winces in pain and pulls out a bloody tooth.)*

Lily: Je peux vous aider? [Can I help you?]

Woman: Who's there? *(They freeze a moment.)* Somebody's here.

Lily: Can I help you?

Woman: Fuck you. Fuck you. Which way did I come from, my left or my right? STAY WHERE YOU ARE! Say it. Just say it: which way?

Lily: Your right.

> *The blind woman rises slowly and turns to her right, tapping ahead. She cries and curses quietly as she exits from where she came. Lily watches her leave, then stares off again. A voice ,Viv (#3), from off SR.*

Viv: Hi.

> *Lily looks off SR again, squints and then smiles weakly.*

Lily: Hello.

Viv: *(Still off.)* I thought it was you...

> *Viv enters. She is a young, attractive woman wearing sunglasses. She is dressed in a white T-shirt on which there is a green hand-painted design. She wears white tights, white Reeboks, has silver bracelets on her forearm and carries a white leather handbag.*

Viv: ...I wasn't sure. You've lost a lot of weight.

Lily: Yes.

Viv: You look great. *(She comes to just right of Lily.)* So, how you doing?

Lily: Ok.

Viv: Haven't seen you in a while. Hot, eh? It's going to pour, I think. You came prepared... You're going to hate me, but I can't remember your name.

Lily: Lily.

Viv: Lily, right, right. I'm useless with names. "You're useless, period..." *(She looks down at the water.)* Fuck, look at that. It's disgusting. Thick with shit. They spend how many millions of dollars hammering fake cobblestones into every street corner and meanwhile look at the water. What's that?

Lily: What?

Viv: That thing there.

Lily: I don't know.

Viv: Yuk.

> *She puts down her handbag and leans on the railing right of Lily. Lily moves her umbrella to her left. Viv removes her sunglasses. Her eyes are very tired.*

Viv: Fuck, it's sticky. I wish it would just rain and be done with it... *(Sings/hums)* "I see my light come shining/ from the west down to the east/ any day now/ any day now/ I shall be released..." Alors je t'ai pas vu au vernissage de Gerty. [So, I didn't see you at Gerty's opening.]

Lily: No.

Viv: L'as tu vu son show? [Have you seen her show?]

Lily: No.

Viv: Ben, t'as une autre semaine pis c'est tout. [Well, you've got one more week and then it's over.] You really should try and see it—you know where we are?

Lily: Yes.

Viv: We moved, eh? On n'est plus sur St. Laurent. [We're not on St. Laurent any more.]

Lily: I know.

Viv: Ok... So what are you doing around here?

Lily: I come here a lot.

Viv: Oh yeah? Me too. Well, I haven't been here in a while. My father used to drag us here, on Sundays, the whole family. "We're going to the locks." Packed us into the car. "Sit still...watch the ships..." He was raised on ships. Ha. He has a wooden leg and a pirate on his shoulder. Ha. Did I say pirate? I meant...yeah. It's too early for jokes, Viv.

> *A seagull cries in the pause.*

Viv: When it rains, in weather like this, it's like it isn't raining, you know what I mean? It's like the rain's not falling. It's just there.

>   *The water laps. Viv hums "I shall be released" as she takes a roll of Life Savers from her bag.*

Viv: Want one? No, eh? I'm addicted to these things. *(She takes one and throws the wrapper into the water. Chews on the candy.)* So, what is it you do, anyway? Do you work?

Lily: No, I'm married.

Viv: Oh, right, right, the little guy. What's his name?

Lily: Gilbert.

Viv: Gilbert, right. He's a banker or something.

Lily: Broker.

Viv: Broker, banker. Bunker, ha. How's he doing?

Lily: He's good. Busy.

Viv: He around here too?

Lily: No.

Viv: Oh, I get it. The Sunday morning argument, right? He got the house.

>   *A wasp flies by her face. She swats at it suddenly.*

Viv: FUCK OFF, YOU! This fucking wasp has been following me since I got here—FUCK OFF! Shoo! Shoo!

>   *The wasp flies to Lily, who swats at it.*

Viv: Aha! It's a male, you can tell. *(The wasp returns to Viv, who swats.)* Shoo! *(They watch it fly off and laugh slightly.)* Wasps. Wasps and seagulls. Have you ever been shit on? Ha, oh, not fun, not fun at all, ha.

>   *During her speech, a man (#1) dressed in black with his shirt open wide passes behind the women from SR to SL, looking at them. Halfway across he swats at a wasp flying by his face. The women, alas, do not notice him.*

Viv: Once, I was going out to dinner with this guy, oh what's his name?... You know him, a little guy, a fag—oh, what's his...he used to have that gallery on St. Denis with the fish... You know him...with the moustache... Anyway, we're going out to dinner, right? We step out of the cab and this seagull drops this enormous turd right on his jacket. Ha, I almost died. Ha. Oh, he was furious—fags hate it when things like that happen, eh? Ha... It was funny because we were going out for seafood... Oh, what was that guy's fucking name?... Anyway... So, Gerty's show is terrific. You really should make the effort to see it. Nature Morte. I love Gerty's still lifes—well, they depress the piss out of me, but I love them. You went to school with Gerty, right?

Lily: Yes.

Viv: That's where I met you. What sort of work do you do? I don't think I've ever...

Lily: I do paintings. Small things.

Viv: Are you the one that does the trains? Gerty was telling me—

Lily: No.

Viv: Trains and bridges—

Lily: No, that's not me.

Viv: Who is that, do you know?

Lily: No.

Viv: I'd like to see that... Oh, did you see that fucking shit, that Georges Ogive guy? At the Centre?

Lily: No.

Viv: So, do you and Gilbert ever go anywhere?

Lily: Well, I've been sick.

Viv: Oh yeah? Anyway, this Ogive guy, oh, it's such a piece of shit—a total rip-off of that guy from New York, what's his name? he did the really big things at the Contemporain two years ago—

Lily: Lewis.

Viv: Lewis, right. That stuff was great, right? So along comes this little faggot two years later and does this watered-down rehash of Lewis' work and it's like the Big Revelation, right? Oh, I hate that, capitalizing on the fact that nobody remembers anything. Bumfuck all the critics et voilà. Le succès de l'année. Fuck. So, what's wrong with you?

Lily: What?

Viv: So, you've been ill. Is that why you lost all that weight?

Lily: Oh, maybe a little, yes.

Viv: So, what is it?

Lily: Oh, it's nothing... Well, I'm...it's nothing serious.

Viv: Well, if being sick makes you look that good... I look like shit today, right? I got like no sleep last night. Oh, last night, last night. I got my period last night. In a cab. I have no cycle, eh? The things just slurps out unexpectedly three or four times a year. I've saved a mint in birth control. Anyway, I'm in a cab, I look down, and blech. My dress was a mess and the poor guy's cab... I didn't have the guts to tell him. What a disaster.

           I went out with this guy last night—well, I've sort of been seeing him on and off—but last night was our first foray into the realm of the senses. He's an older guy, a lot older, ha. A dentist—lots of money. Very distinguished looking. Divorced looking, you look at him and you know he's divorced. We met at a party at my parents' place, for Christ's sake. He shows up at the gallery the next day, takes me out, spoils me to death. I'm so stupid. I don't really like the guy, you know, he's all right. Well, you want to take me out and spend lots of money on me, fine—I'm going to refuse? Anyway, this has been going on, I don't know, a month, two months. So last night he takes me out to see this play—real piece of shit—some intense family drama about life in rural Canada; it literally took place in the kitchen. So afterwards we go for sushi and we're eating and drinking and he, he starts talking all seriously, you know? He's never talked like...I mean, up to now it's been a lot of small talk, but tonight, tonight it's the full treatment. The Divorce, and a long time on that one. The sense of failure. Thirty years as a dentist. He said...he said, I feel like I have been standing still watching my life walk past me. Yeah...

And I don't want to hear this stuff, right? I mean, I'm doing well—no, that's not what I mean. I mean, it's all right to have some nice chit-chat over dinner and then watch him puff around the dance floor, but I don't want to hear this stuff about failure. So I'm drinking as much as he'll pay for, right? And I'm saying these obnoxious things, making smart-ass remarks about everything he says and I can tell I'm hurting his feelings, but I can't stop myself and he's trying to pretend like it's not bothering him.

Anyway, we go to his place and you have to see this place. His wife got the house, right? So, he's bought himself this renovated condo on St. Paul, but he's decorated it all Japanese with no chairs, just these cushions on the floor and the midget tables and the erotic drawings. And the piano. And on the piano there's this photo of a woman, like a real knock-out, so I ask, "Who's this? Another conquest?" "No," he says, "that's my daughter." She's older than me, right? She's a lawyer.

So we're on the floor, and he's talking all serious again and I could tell he was really nervous, which really bugged me for some reason. It's because...well, I'm starting to realize that he really likes me. And he's opening his heart and I'm making fun of him and I can see he's hurt, but I can't stop... Finally I kissed him just to shut myself up.

But it was worse in bed. First of all, he's really nervous or he comes from strange old school of fucking I've never heard of. And taking this big tired old dick into your mouth... Touching him was weird, his back... I mean, he has a really good body for a guy his age... He tried to drag an orgasm out of me, practically tore my boobs off at one point.

Anyway, it's over and I'm hoping I can sleep, but no, it starts— you know when guys talk late at night? They're so glad it's dark and you can't see them and they take out this quiet little voice—they all have that same voice—and they tell you how the world has misinterpreted their dreams.

But I couldn't stay awake. I started having this dream. It was weird: I was on a beach, it was winter, it was really cold, it's night and I'm on this beach watching this turtle, this huge turtle dragging itself towards the sea.

Then he asks me a question, but I'm watching my turtle, right? So I say WHAT? And he laughs and hugs me and I thought "Oh, no, he wants to fuck me again" but he didn't. He just gives me a kiss on the forehead, says good night and rolls over.

But now I can't sleep. I started trembling all over, I couldn't stop. I didn't want him to notice, but the more I tried to stop, the worse it got and he asks "Is anything wrong?" and I spring from the bed. I just made it to the can. I puked my guts out. And I'm in his bathroom, naked, wiping the rim of the bowl with toilet paper and the light comes on and I yell "TURN IT OFF" and it dies. And my eyes get used to the dark and this silhouette of an old naked man is in the doorway asking "Are you all right?"

Then it's me running around getting dressed, trying not to look at him in his kimono and saying things like "Don't worry. This happens all the time. I have a sensitive stomach." And he wants to drive me home and I insist no. Finally the cab comes and he gives me the money for it.

And I'm going home and the sun is coming up and I start bleeding all over this cab, right? And I couldn't sleep. And I'm washing out my dress and around ten the phone rings and I know it's him. It rang like fifty times. I was still ringing when I left the apartment. Poor guy. So, how long have you known Gilbert?

Lily:　　　Eleven years.

Viv:　　　Eleven years? Where'd you meet?

Lily:　　　In high school.

Viv:　　　You've been with him since high school? What, he's like your first boyfriend? Eleven years... And you've never cheated on him or anything.

Lily:　　　I have.

Viv: Oh yeah? You don't talk much, do you?

Lily: Well, I was alone. I was thinking. Whenever I talk, nobody
            understands what I'm talking about.

            *Viv looks at Lily for a moment. Then both stare out, lost in their
            own thoughts. Water sounds, a gull. Lily absently runs a hand
            under her blouse and holds her left breast. Absolute stillness.
            Viv suddenly notices the thing in the water.*

Viv: Oh my god, it's a dog.

Lily: What?

Viv: The thing in the water. It's been there for days probably.

            *They stare at the dead dog. It begins to rain. Lily opens her
            umbrella. Viv grabs her bag and stands under the umbrella
            with Lily. They look at the dog.*

Viv: Hey, I just realized: this is Father's Day, isn't it?

SEAGULL/HER

A brief choreography. The music begins first, then the lights. Projected film: a snowstorm on an ocean beach. The film projected through a green filter. Within this film is the stage action.

The story is simple. A bird with a large branch in its mouth (#5) crosses the stage. He drops the branch when a woman in green (#4) rises from the stage floor. They dance together briefly, then the gull assumes the waki position, kneeling extreme DSL.

The woman dances a story of a broken love affair. It ends furiously with the woman exhausted. The gull, who has been watching, raises a branch. It burns briefly. The gull's hand also burns briefly and then the light dies on him, leaving only the woman facing front. The light dies on her. The music fades.

AND

One dim bare green bulb over centre stage. Actors #1-4 sit huddled on a bench against the wall USL. All are dressed in black. All stare at a tiny scraggy Christmas tree on the floor before them. Eric Satie's "Vexations" plays quietly throughout the piece.

A man (#5) enters slowly from USR to CS beneath the dim bulb and faces the audience. He wears the black trenchcoat of Man (#1) in Rabbit, *regardless of the fit. During his speech the other actors utter the occasional quiet "no."*

Man: And it's the dead of winter. All in the same boat...adrift in the middle of some cold ocean...some sea.

The four others are dead...and I'm next...maybe I'll send up a flare.

It's Christmas Eve—a storm rising green and black. I'll be dead soon, so I tell myself a story...adrift, falling in my father's footsteps.

It's Christmas Eve...Christ's birthday...Christ...was a Capricorn...a goat...born of a barn stinking of donkeys... reindeer turds steaming on your roof...a scorched fat man suffocates in your chimney...it's Christmas Eve and I...am in...a mall...and I am waiting my turn at an automatic teller. It's Christmas Eve, 5:05 pm, and I have not yet bought my wife a Christmas present. I'm next at the teller...I'm next. Mistletoe dangles over the machine...the guy at the machine now looks like Santa—a fat bearded baldy in a red Kanuk...what would have happened if they nailed up old Saint Nick instead at Easter time? Santa's done, counting his cash under the mistletoe. He looks at me...no, I do not want to kiss him.

And it's my turn at the machine...what's my balance? Dick. And in the chequing account?... Not available. I'll take out cash on the credit card. And I'm adrift in the mall.

I'm in Eaton's...purses...there are many purses...I am surrounded by hanging purses...I have never seen so many purses...this is a lot of purses...does she need—no, she has a purse.

And I'm adrift up an escalator into the toy department. It's a shambles, all but empty and at my feet there's a doll half torn from her box. I try to stuff her back in...nope...the box is fucked. "Do you intend on buying that, sir?"—the saleslady came from nowhere...she's glaring at me and her mouth is...pursed. "If you don't want it, that's no reason to destroy it." She snatches it from me. "No, I was trying to...the box is all..." and she walks away.

And I'm sitting at a donut stand in the middle of the mall—the donut stand is a giant donut with a bite taken out of it...to get inside the donut you have to go through a little door in the bite...I am sitting by the bite, having a very bad cup of coffee and a very bad donut. What time is it? 5:40. I remember 5:40...I remember 5:40 a year ago...I remember 5:40 a year ago, a coffee and a donut...I remember 5:40 a year ago, a coffee and a donut at the hospital cafeteria...I was watching the second hand...and she was upstairs having the abortion.

And it's 5:50—what am I going to get her? Perfume? ...bullshit. A book?...that's romantic. Another cocksucking sweater? A clock radio? What's this? That's cute: a pickled person...a little person in a jar...a pickled person...a little smiling face pressed up against the glass...no.

And it's six o'clock...the stores are dead...and I have nothing.

And I go out to the parking lot...the snowstorm has started, but the snow isn't falling...it's rising...

And I walk to my car and I start my car and my car warms up and I have nothing...Jesus...what am I going to tell her? Maybe I can stop by a Jean Coutu. They'll be open till nine.

Treat me like a fool...why are you drawing bunnies?...and

nothing means anything...and I start bleeding all over this cab, right?...a seagull and a girl in green...falling in my father's footsteps...these foolish things swirl up in my head as my car warms up...and they will go on swirling after I'm dead...never to begin again...only to continue.

And I put the car in drive and I step on the gas and the back wheel spins...and I'm not moving. I am stuck in a snowbank...a...drift.

And the wheel spins.

And I'm not moving.

And the snow swirls up.

And it will all go on.

And the wheel spins.

And I'm not moving.

And

The End